Labour's Plan

Outlined by Harold Wilson

Selected Speeches 1964

Penguin Books

Penguin Books Ltd, Harmondsworth,
Middlesex, England
Penguin Books Pty Ltd, Ringwood, Victoria,
Australia

First published 1964

Made and printed in Great Britain
by C. Nicholls & Company Ltd
Set in Monotype Times

The Rt Hon. Harold Wilson, O.B.E., M.P. was born in
1916 and educated on scholarships at Royds Hall
Secondary School, Huddersfield, Wirral Grammar
School, Cheshire, and Jesus College, Oxford where he
obtained an outstanding First in P.P.E. At twenty-one
he became a lecturer in Economics at New College,
Oxford, and research assistant to Lord Beveridge. A
year later he went to University College as a Fellow.
During the war he was in the Civil Service, and was
Director of Economics and Statistics from 1943 to
1944, when he was elected to Parliament, becoming
Parliamentary Secretary to the Ministry of Works.
In 1947 he was appointed Secretary for Overseas
Trade. He later succeeded Sir Stafford Cripps as
President of the Board of Trade. In 1950 he was
re-elected to Parliament for Huyton, Lancashire, which
he has represented ever since. He resigned from the
Board of Trade in 1951 in protest against government
policy on health charges and armament expenditure.
In 1960 he contested the Labour Party leadership with
Hugh Gaitskell, but was defeated; he was elected
leader in 1963. From 1954 he has been a member of the
'Shadow Cabinet' and from 1955 to 1961 he was
responsible for shaping the Labour Party's financial and
economic policy. In 1961 he was assigned the
responsibility of leading his Party on foreign affairs.
He has visited many countries, including the United
States and Russia, on various missions, and has had
talks with Kennedy, Johnson, and Khrushchev.
Harold Wilson is married and has two sons.

The New Britain

Contents

Preface

The speeches in this book were for the most part made in a nation-wide pre-election-speaking campaign undertaken between January and April 1964. They are printed as delivered, save for the deletion of purely topical political references, such as challenges to hold an early election and replies to speeches made concurrently by Conservative leaders.

Each speech, apart from the first and last, was designed to present the Labour Party's policy on a specific subject. Chapter 1, on building the New Britain, portrayed the kind of society we wish to see in Britain and the steps that will have to be taken to create it. Chapter 2, 'Labour's Economic Policy', sets out in considerable detail our economic and financial policy; Chapter 3, 'A First-Class Nation', the measures designed to modernize British industry and to apply the fruits of scientific and technological research to industrial processes; Chapter 4, 'Housing and Planning', our proposals for housing, urban regeneration, and regional planning; and Chapter 5, 'Plan for Full Employment', our proposals for employment policy and the diversification of industry.

Chapter 9, made at a mass rally at the Royal Albert Hall, to mark the end of the spring campaign, drew together the threads of the earlier speeches and summarized the aims of the future in terms of social purpose, economic purpose, and Britain's purpose in the world.

In addition to the six speeches made at public meetings, Chapters 6 to 8 reprint further speeches made during the same period. Chapter 6, 'Law Reform and the Citizen', was an address given at a meeting in the Niblett Hall, Inner Temple, to the Society of Labour Lawyers. Chapter 7 was an address on foreign affairs made at the University of Bridgeport, Connecticut, on the occasion of my visit to the United States to meet President Johnson. Chapter 8, 'Plan for the Commonwealth', was a speech made in the House of Commons debate on the Future of the Commonwealth, on 6 February.

Speeches are made to be heard, and as a rule do not read well. These will no doubt prove no exception to that rule, but the invitation by Penguin Books to me to assemble them for publication in convenient book form will, I hope, ensure that all who are concerned with the vital national issues which confront Britain in 1964 are provided with the means of reading where the Labour Party stands.

HOUSE OF COMMONS
June 1964

1　The New Britain

A speech made at the Town Hall, Birmingham, on Sunday, 19 January 1964

I want to speak to you today about a new Britain and how we intend to bring home to our people the excitement there will be in building it.

For 1964 is the year in which we can take our destiny into our own hands again.

Since the war, the world has been rushing forward at an unprecedented, an exhilarating speed. In two decades, the scientists have made more progress than in the past two thousand years. They have made it possible for man to reach out to the stars, and to bring abundance from the earth. They have made it possible to end the dark ages of poverty and want, to take mankind forward to a future which our fathers could not have dreamed possible. Yet Britain lags behind, lacking the will or the plan which can bring this future within the reach of all.

The reason is not far to seek. We are living in the jet-age but we are governed by an Edwardian establishment mentality. Over the British people lies the chill frost of Tory leadership. They freeze initiative and petrify imagination. They cling to privilege and power for the few, shutting the gates on the many. Tory society is a *closed* society, in which birth and wealth have priority, in which the master-and-servant, landlord-and-tenant mentality is predominant. The Tories have proved that they are incapable of mobilizing Britain to take full advantage of the scientific breakthrough. Their approach and methods are fifty years out of date.

Labour wants to mobilize the entire nation in the nation's business. It wants to create government of the whole people by the whole people. Labour will replace the closed, exclusive society by an open society in which all have an opportunity to work and serve, in which brains will take precedence over blue-blood, and craftsmanship will be more important than caste. Labour wants to streamline our institutions, modernize methods of government, bring the entire nation into a working partnership with the state.

Only by this national mobilization of all our resources of energy, manpower, brains, imagination, and skill can Britain get the effort which is needed to take us through to a new age of fulfilment. Let us not talk, as the Prime Minister did at the Mansion House, of a pussy-footing one per cent more: it is a 100 per cent we want. And we can get it.

This is the time for a breakthrough to an exciting and wonderful period in our history, in which all can and must take part. Our young men and women, especially, have in their hands the power to change the world. We want the youth of Britain to storm the new frontiers of knowledge, to bring back to Britain that surging adventurous self-confidence and sturdy self-respect which the Tories have almost submerged by their apathy and cynicism.

The great weakness of the Conservatives is their failure to try to represent the nation. We do not believe that a small minority of the British people, distinguished by their family connexions, or educational background, have a unique right to positions of influence and power. We believe that Britain's future depends on the thrusting ability and even iconoclasm of millions of products of our grammar schools, comprehensive schools, technical schools and colleges, secondary moderns, and the rest, who are today held down not only within the Government Party but over a wide sector of industry.

This is what 1964 can mean. A chance for change. More, a time for resurgence. A chance to sweep away the grouse-moor conception of Tory leadership and refit Britain with a new image, a new confidence. A chance to change the face and future of Britain.

What is it that we want to change? It is not the enduring values which have made Britain great, it is not the qualities of independence and personal freedom, the democratic right of dissent, the right to argue. What we want to change is the clammy unimaginativeness at the top, which has prevented our people exercising these qualities and energies in full measure.

The fault lies not in our people, but in the form and pattern in which our national system of government has come to be ordered. Let me say what I think is wrong, and what it is we have to change.

(1) As a nation, we have missed many of the opportunities offered to us by the scientific revolution – because we have had a Government which this scientific age has passed by; because we have not trained the scientists and engineers we need; because we have an industrial system, large parts of which are constitutionally incapable of applying the discoveries of science to factory processes. The scientists and engineers who have left Britain have voted already in this election: they have voted with their feet.

(2) There has been a complete failure to plan ahead for the future. Annual budgets, short-term programmes, feverish little election spurts – there has been no vision of the Britain we are seeking to create.

(3) Our industrial system is held down, stagnating, every spurt of expansion followed by crisis and long periods of restriction.

(4) At every level of our national life, talent and ability are wasted; our children do not get equal opportunities or our citizens equal chances to develop their qualities and energies.

(5) In an age of great potential plenty, we are still in this country cursed by indefensible pockets of shameful poverty and injustice which twelve years of so-called affluence have not removed.

(6) Many of our institutions and our processes, governmental and local government, for decision-making are clumsy, amateurish, ineffective, and out-of-date.

(7) In a world which I believe is genuinely looking to Britain for a lead which no others can give, our misgovernment has reduced our influence to a level far below that justified by our inherent national skill and, I believe, our national idealism.

(8) At a time when so many good causes – Freedom from Hunger, Oxfam, War on Want – have shown the passionate desire of our people to do something for others, the Government's lack of direction, lack of imagination, lack of inspiration

has failed to give the dynamic lead to which our people would have responded.

If these are the things to be changed, what sort of new Britain is it that we want to create?

I would put it like this.

(1) We want a Britain in which all of us feel that we are part of a new policy-making, of taking national decisions, where every home, every club, every pub is its own Parliament-in-miniature, thrashing out the issues of the day. We want a Britain where ideas and the efforts of its citizens are more important to the Government than day-to-day ups and downs in public opinion polls or on the stock exchange.

(2) We want a Britain whose motivation is not private profit and the aggrandizement of personal fortunes but national effort and national purpose – a responsible Britain based on public service, not a commercialized society where everything has its price.

(3) We want to see a Britain which faces its difficulties frankly and fully, which does not pretend that what has to be done can easily be done, which rescues our national life from the disillusionment of the promises dishonestly given, naïvely accepted, and too often the product of a cyclical electoral philosophy.

(4) We want a Britain in which the Government picks the best brains in the land and harnesses them to the task of national regeneration.

(5) We want a Britain that truly believes in itself, in its power to make its own future, dictated to by none, but willing to play its full part in the Commonwealth, in the U.N., and in the alliances which we regard as essential for peace.

(6) This means that we want a Britain, not conservative, nostalgic, backward-looking, but proud of its past and willing to rediscover the true traditions of our nation as a guide to our role in the future: because the real traditions of Britain are not to be found in the so-called qualities that have been exalted and disproportionately rewarded in these past few years. It was our people's ingenuity, innovation, sometimes their brashness and saltiness, and political irreverence, our energy, determination, and merchant-adventuring spirit which gave us our influence in

the world. Nothing so perverts our national life as Conservative attempts to identify the British standard of independence, ingenuity, and venture with the self-interest of the share pushers, take-over bidders, land and property speculators, and ad-mass extravagances.

(7) In short, we want a Britain that believes in its power to make a distinctive and decisive contribution to the world, a Britain that breaks down the barriers of colour and class – of occupation, skill, and age – which, by dividing our economic life between the power élite on the one hand and the technicians, scientists, and production men on the other, prevents this nation from realizing its full potential.

Now why do we feel that the present Government cannot build this new Britain?

Why? First, of course, because in nearly thirteen years they have not done so. No one will be misled by their last-minute repentance on the eve of an election. We had this before in 1955, and in 1959, and in neither case did it long survive the counting of the votes.

Secondly, the Conservative Party, except at election time, are never willing to renounce their sectional approach to the extent needed to build the kind of Britain we all want. I make no personal attack on their leaders or M.P.s, who are not themselves selfish or greedy, or deliberately desirous of sacrificing the broader national interest to private gain. Our attack is on their philosophy, not least in times of national crisis, a philosophy which identifies the national interest with the interests of those who make money rather than of those who earn money, with, if you like, speculation rather than industry. Their reluctance, indeed, refusal, to make public the source of their electoral funds enhances the suspicions that in any assessment of the true national interest they are not entirely their own masters.

In foreign affairs, they are obsessed with a nostalgia for past grandeur, with a feeling that the world owes us a living, and that some international old-boy network will take charge and see us through. They fail to realize that national influence is a function of our economic strength and independence, and of a defence policy related not to prestige illusions but to the hard facts and realization of our situation and the world in which we live.

At home and abroad, they are out of touch with the age in which we live, amiable coelocanths no longer suited to the waters which lap the shores of the world in which we are living.

So what must be done to build a new Britain?

We must face the real world as it is, identify its dangers and opportunities, and make some estimate of its future trends so that, as a nation, we can sometimes anticipate events and not be overwhelmed by them.

We must shape our policies at home and abroad as part of an administrative unity.

This is what Socialism means, a unity of direction for all the decisions a government has to take; because we shall not achieve this Britain, except on a basis of a purposeful unity of our policies. This means for a start, planning. Just as the Government have, belatedly and unsurely, and perhaps not permanently, begun to apply the techniques of appraisal, and quantitative analysis, even of statistical projection, to the problem of economic expansion, so we have to approach all our other problems – colonial, foreign, defence, no less than town planning and transport – on clear and courageous assessments of objectives, resources, and priorities. And in this whole field, of affairs at home and abroad, no less than in industry and science and technology, we have to cease this affectation of amateurism, we have to cease this pretence that somehow you are better than other people if you go into the M.C.C. by the Gentlemen's gate and not by the Players'. We have got to recognize that at every level the trained mind, the trained hand, the professional will be needed.

Socialism, as I understand it, means applying a sense of purpose to our national life: economic purpose, social purpose, and moral purpose. Purpose means technical skill – be it the skill of a manager, a designer, a craftsman, an engineer, a transport worker, a miner, an architect, a nuclear physicist, a doctor, a nurse, or a social worker. If you fly the Atlantic in a jet, you want to be sure the pilot knows his job, that he's been trained for it. If you're in hospital, you feel more confident if you know that the surgeon has given his lifetime to fitting himself for his work.

Pilot or surgeon: it matters not who his father was, or what school he went to, or who his friends are. Yet in Government and in business we are still too often content to accept social qualifications rather than technical ability as the criterion.

But this is not to equate, as our opponents affect to do, Socialism with technocracy. The essential leavening which Socialism brings to the industrial revolution of our age is the leavening of humanity, which was so clearly absent from Britain's first industrial revolution.

So we shall need in this highly organized age to protect the public interest against the ever-increasing high-pressure strategy of private interests, and we shall open up opportunities for everyone. Ability must be the test, and ability is not to be measured by upper-class accents; in the modern world it is the quality of ruggedness not smoothness that we need.

We must reconstruct our institutions to make us capable of courageous decision-making and of evoking the spirit of national partnership that will be required. This means a new sense of drive in the higher direction of our national affairs; it means changes in our departmental structure to reflect the scientific and technological realities of the new age; it means a degree of decentralization, for not all wisdom abides in London; it means the creation of regional organs of Government.

It is bad enough for the thrust of our people to be frustrated by the vested interests and institutions of a dead past.

This then is the choice the country will have to make: between the old Britain to which the Tories cling or the new democratic Britain which we plan to build.

More and more, during the next few weeks, we shall stress the detailed policies which we intend to follow. *Signposts for the Sixties*, endorsed by the Party Conference by an overwhelming majority, sets out the main lines of our policy, and this, of course, we have supplemented with more detailed statements over the past two years.

I have said that our election campaign will cover three main issues: economic purpose, social purpose, and the standing of Britain in the world.

On economic purpose, all our plans for raising living standards in Britain and for playing our full part in the world war against poverty and hunger will come to naught unless we can replace the stop-go economic policy of this Government with a studied and sustained economic expansion. Next week at Swansea in the second of this series of meetings, I hope to spend a considerable amount of time going into the details of how this is going to be achieved.

We have said many times what will be involved. We believe in planning. Long before the Conservatives had announced their conversion to the principles of N.E.D.C., we had produced a Four-Year Plan for Britain, figures and all, based on a vigorous programme of expanding capital investment in plant, machinery, and buildings, based too on a purposive expansion of export – and import-saving industries. This will be at the centre of our programme. For the basic cause of the stop-go economy has been the fact that as soon as home production begins to expand, in your pre-election boom, imports rise and exports fall off.

We believe that this purposive expansion cannot be achieved without radical changes in our taxation system designed to encourage the enterprising and to penalize the slothful and in-efficient within British industry. These tax changes will mean, too, a fairer fiscal system ensuring that those vast accumulations of wealth which today avoid tax shall bear their fair share.

We believe that expansion cannot be achieved either, without the proposals we have put forward for our basic industries – public ownership of steel, and an integrated plan for transport, to replace the piecemeal policies of the Beeching approach. Nor shall we be able to recapture our lost ground in world markets without new publicly owned industries based on the scientific revolution. And this in its turn requires a new national emphasis on a different kind of investment, investment not in plant and machinery and buildings, but investment in human beings, above all through radical and dynamic changes in our educational system.

At present, as recent reports have shown, half the talent, energy, and drive of this nation is going to waste, as the result of our vicious system of so-called élite education. After a decade and more of Tory rule we have, it is true, first-rate educational opportunities for the minority of children, who can break through to the universities and to other higher-education institutions. But what the Conservatives have completely failed to provide are the funds and the drive required to give first-rate education to the majority of our children who crowd the classes of very often dingy primary and secondary modern schools and are shoved out on the labour market at the age of fifteen.

Having skimped the education of all but the clever minority, or the fortunate minority, for years, the Government has now tried to demonstrate its faith in education by conceding the right of every child who can benefit by it to go to a university, which is the central principle of the Robbins Report. The Government take credit for accepting the Robbins Report, for accepting now what we have been saying for years. Well then, why after thirteen years is the proportion of those who show their fitness in A-level examinations and then get to university actually declining? I remember the debate, one of Hugh Gaitskell's greatest speeches in April 1962, less than two years ago, on the University Grants Committee. I remember in that debate when the Tories, crisis-bound, were still saying we couldn't afford three or four million pounds more for university expansion, and when all the great modernizers of today tramped through the division lobbies to deny those millions to university expansion.

But may I say that, unlike them, we in the Labour Party are not content to substitute an eighteen-plus for the eleven-plus and lavish all our care on the fifteen boys and girls out of a hundred who can hope to get a place in a university. To make the best of our brilliant scientists is vital, but it is just as important to do what we can for our great army of technicians, craftsmen, and skilled workers. One thing at least Robbins has accepted: they have accepted our demand that we should end snobbery in higher education. They have accepted our view that if you increase the numbers going forward for higher education you won't be debasing the quality, because there are a lot more to come, there are a lot more to show what they can do. And equally we believe that nothing but the best is good enough when it comes to the training of our school-leavers who go into industry and commerce. We intend to pay just as much attention to the needs of the apprentice at the tech as we do to the needs of the undergraduate at Oxford and Cambridge. Because our future depends just as much on the one as on the other.

All this will mean priorities, and we shall not hesitate in the field of building, where existing programmes and promises already threaten to overload the building and civil engineering industries – we shall not hesitate to decide that less essential projects – not least, speculative office building and the like – shall if necessary be held back to give priority projects the right of way.

'Controls', the Tories will say; but there are controls today: every time the Minister of Education cuts your local authority school building programme, which he does with unfailing regularity, you have a control; there are controls over essential buildings. We for our part are prepared to have controls over less essential building, so that the essential building can go ahead. And the controls we shall not be afraid to impose, are the controls of starting dates, and phasing in time. These controls will be necessary if even the national priorities announced by the Conservatives are to be observed.

Nor, again, shall we be able to achieve a sustained expansion programme unless we have a national incomes policy based on social justice. The Conservatives come forward with last-minute proposals designed more for their electoral effect than for economic strength and solvency. At the Labour Party Conference in Scarborough we adopted by a huge majority a policy of planned growth of income related to national productivity, and the need for this was recognized by every trade-union leader who came to the rostrum.

We in the Labour Party have the right to ask for this policy because we are willing to create the conditions in which it can be established – conditions applying to *all* incomes, not just wages; all incomes, not excluding rents; because we realize the essential unity of social policy and incomes strategy; because we can come to the two sides of industry with clean hands, with no responsibility for the faith-breaking interference with collective bargaining and industrial conciliation and arbitration that was involved in Mr Selwyn Lloyd's pay pause.

And *we* can make the national appeal that is needed because, for us, an incomes policy is the condition of sustained growth and because a pledge of sustained growth is a condition of that policy. In the past twelve years, the Conservatives have repeatedly sought to impose a pay freeze because a stagnant economy, indeed an economy forcibly prevented from expanding, could not pay higher wages without inflation. We therefore have the right to talk of a national incomes policy.

So too with social purpose. We are proud of the social purpose that has built up this Movement. In the 1960s when we are putting forward policies relevant to the age in which we live, relevant to the age of automation, of jet and space travel, it is still as true as it ever was that the fundamental inspiration of our social life should be the age-old Socialist principle: from each according to his means, to each according to his needs. And we are all of us proud to think that the new social proposals that we are going to put before the electorate in the forthcoming election still reflect that great Socialist principle.

The pioneers of our movement were levellers, centuries ago, but they believed in levelling up, not in levelling down. When, for example, they said that security was a privilege of wealth, they were not seized by an envious passion for destruction. Instead, they resolved to transform this private security into a social security and make it not the privilege of a few but the right of every citizen.

Our National Health Service, the creation of one of the greatest socialists who ever lived, was founded on this simple principle – that the best medical care should no longer be obtainable only by those who could pay for private treatment and the nursing home, but made available to everyone, whatever his means. Our system of national social security – introduced by another great socialist, Jim Griffiths – applies this principle in yet another field, by ensuring that decent living standards in sickness, in widowhood, and in old age should be assured not only to those with private means but to every employed worker and his family.

Conservative policy throughout these past years, these years that are now coming to an end, has denied and eroded this principle, so that the means test, which the first Labour Government began to abolish, has been made a built-in part of Tory social security. More than two million old people today are forced to submit themselves to a means test in order to obtain the minimum living standard provided by National Assistance. We have put forward, and our Conference has endorsed, a plan for ending this scandal. In the long run, our system of graded benefits and graded pensions will ensure half-pay in retirement, in sickness and old age, to the average paid worker, and rather more than half-pay at somewhat reduced contributions to those whose earnings are at the lower end of the scale. As for the urgent problems of existing pensioners, one of our first acts will be to introduce what we call the 'income guarantee', a guaranteed minimum income available to them all. And this over the period we have in mind will lift the vast majority of those two million who are now forced to accept the means test well above the level of National Assistance.

So the extent of need, not the size of personal wealth, will be the passport to social security. There will be no incantations about 'never having it so good' until we have dealt with the pockets of real poverty in this country. And you won't find a Labour Government claiming that this country would be bankrupt if we provided a few invacars for the war-disabled or for paraplegic ex-miners at a time when it can offer, on expense accounts, to provide expensive cars by the thousand.

And it is, finally, no good talking about the standard of living until we are prepared to tackle the housing problem. Far more houses built to let – and this won't be achieved until we have tackled the land problem and until we have put into force our Socialist plans to guarantee reasonable interest rates to local authorities for their house-building programmes. More houses, and on more reasonable terms for owner-occupiers – these won't be achieved, either, until we have tackled the land scandal and the problem of interest rates. Fair rents and security against evictions – these won't be achieved until we have repealed the Rent Act and replaced it with a measure giving justice to landlord and tenant, and putting an end to evictions. Modernization of old rented houses – this won't be achieved until we use the powers we intend to use, and until we have smoked out the last relics of Rachmanism and anonymous landlordism from our towns and cities. For twelve years the Tories have sought to solve the housing problem on the basis that it can be and should be an instrument for private profit. We believe that it cannot be solved until it is treated as a social service, as a problem of priorities, until we have taken the profit out of land speculation by the community itself owning the land on which the buildings have got to be put up, and until we have geared our national interest rate policy to social needs.

Last of all, Britain's standing in the world. This will never be assured until we have fortified our economic strength at home, until we have reshaped our defence policy on the basis of hard facts and world realities, until we have decided the purposes for which our voice is to be heard in the world.

For years, Britain has been found ranged too often with the reactionary elements – the South African and Portuguese colonial regimes – instead of ridding the world of racialism and oppression. Shortsightedness and a wrong calculation of economic advantage have caused this country to turn its back on the Commonwealth, wherein lies not only our economic strength but our potential for world leadership.

The last time I talked in this Hall, at the beginning of May [1963], I repeated, in case the Tory Government and Tory press were in any doubt, the pledge I had given in Trafalgar Square about our determination to impose an arms embargo on South Africa. That speech in Birmingham led to further attacks and further smears from Tory Ministers and the Tory press. But by the end of July Labour's policy was the policy of the United States of America. By the end of July it was the policy of the United Nations. By the end of August the British Government were trying to pretend it had been their policy all along.

So, then, economic purpose, social purpose, world purpose: these are the issues on which we shall be fighting. All that this means in terms of our detailed policies I hope to outline more fully in the remaining speeches of this present campaign. Your task and mine are clear: it is to bring home to every one of our fellow-electors the distinctive Socialist issues on which we shall be fighting the election when it comes; issues reflecting the faith and ideals that created this movement; issues which in this dynamic, scientific age are more relevant than they have ever been – the challenge facing Britain in the world in which we live; the issues, in short, which are involved in building our new, Socialist Britain.

A speech delivered at the Brangwyn Hall, Swansea, on
Saturday, 25 January 1964

... Last week, I spoke about our vision of a New Britain. Tonight,
I want to say how it can be guaranteed. There is one way only: it
depends on our national production.

Why do we give such a high priority to expanding production?
The answer is that all else in our programmes and our vision for
the new Britain depend on what we turn out from our factories,
mines, and farms; our laboratories and our drawing offices.

On our national production effort depends our standing in the
world. Our influence abroad has been crippled by low production
which has put us periodically in pawn. Never has our influence
been weaker than in the period when a Conservative Government,
bankrupt of any ideas for regenerating our economy, looked to
the Common Market to solve all our economic problems. When
Ministers were urging their followers to support entry on almost
any terms, when even the Prime Minister could say on a national
television broadcast that we are nothing without Europe, then
we could see the urgent need for policies to build up our strength.

On our national productive effort, too, rests our ability to help
the people in Africa and Asia and other parts of the world in the
life and death struggle against poverty and hunger, against
illiteracy and disease.

Again, all our plans for raising our national production provide the basis for achieving and maintaining full employment,
for raising living standards in our own country, ending the
shameful pockets of poverty which disfigure our society; the
basis too for our plans to fight ill-health and disease, to transform
our educational system from its present two-nation orientation
to a system sparkling with opportunity. Everything depends on a
firm basis of economic power. Expanding production was at

once the assumption and the inspiration of our Scarborough programme.

It is, of course, equally an essential assumption in the Conservative catalogue of election promises – for what we have seen in the past three months has been a prodigious and, by Conservative standards, uncharacteristic list of expenditure commitments, all pledging our future national income on the assumption of continued economic growth.

The interesting thing is that all these last-minute election pledges are in fields of expenditure where, only recently, the Government, oppressed by the limits placed on them by their own sacrosanct stop-go policy, told us that the nation could not afford the social advance that we were demanding.

I remember the 1959 election when one of the main themes of Conservative counter-attack was the assertion that Britain could not afford Labour's programmes of social reform. 'Why,' said Lord Hailsham, 'to carry out all the Socialists are promising would increase expenditure by up to £800 millions a year in the new Parliament.' £1,000 millions was Mr Macmillan's overbid. In the event, the Conservatives have increased expenditure, not by £800 millions a year, but, on last year's estimates, by £1,800 millions. And their latest expenditure White Paper talks of increasing national expenditure by a further £1,900 millions.

They have now accepted the argument Hugh Gaitskell and the rest of us put forward in 1959 that Britain can shoulder these necessary commitments if, and only if, we are able to keep production growing year by year.

I have no desire to belittle the extent of their conversion.

1. Less than two years ago we demanded a few millions more for urgently needed university expansion. No, said the Government, we can't afford it. Now they suddenly pledge themselves to an additional £3,500 millions over ten years.

2. Three years ago we called for more council houses. No, said Sir Keith Joseph, they're not needed. In 1963 he announces a boost in council house building.

3. Year after year we pressed for local authorities to be able to borrow at reasonable rates through the Public Works Loans Board. No, said the Government, bad financial doctrine. Last

week we had the Bill enabling local councils to borrow through the Public Works Loans Board.

4. Year after year, we called for the planning of food imports. No, said the Ministry of Agriculture, this would mean food rationing. In December 1963 a Bill to regulate food imports appears.

5. *Signposts for the Sixties* outlined our plan for taking urban building land into public ownership. Unworkable, rank Socialism, said the Tories. Now they say, 'me too'.

6. Fight the evils of Rachmanism, we said, last July. A political stunt, said Sir Keith Joseph; besides the councils have all the powers they need. Then, in November, they produced a Bill to give the councils powers to fight Rachmanism – so far as they went.

7. Speed up the work of the Monopolies Commission, we said. Not necessary, said the President of the Board of Trade. Now the Commission is to be given more powers and to be speeded up.

So one could go on with case after case where the approach of the election has brought them to announce, as with a blinding revelation, their support of Labour policies they had condemned. If the Conservatives have one theme song for their election campaign, it should be 'Little Sir Echo'.

At least, in the next election, we shall not have the Tory red herring that Britain cannot afford to pay for the programmes we need to regenerate Britain's social life and end the degrading contrast between private affluence and public squalor. The argument in the next election will not be whether we can afford these programmes. Both sides now realize that we cannot afford to reject them. The argument will be this: can the Conservatives or Labour best galvanize our sluggish, fitful economy?

Why, Aneurin Bevan asked, look into the crystal when you can read the book?

Under Britain's post-war Labour Government we had a steady increase in production surpassing all our main industrial rivals. Under the Conservatives, the 4 per cent annual increase which they have now so glibly accepted has been achieved in only, at most, three of the last twelve years. It is true that every four or five years a deliberately engineered consumption boom is generated which, after a few months, calls forth spectacular increases in national production. But the very nature of an artificial and ephemeral stimulus of this kind soon causes crisis. The basic infrastructure of Tory economic society soon succumbs to insupportable strains. A rapidly expanding home market exerts a dangerous pull on exports; a disproportionate rise in imports is needed to feed our factories and shops. So the green light changes to amber, interest rates rise, social programmes are cut back, and within a year the red light of economic crisis – with 7 per cent bank rates, additional taxation, and cuts in social expenditure – bring the economy grinding to a halt.

Of course, now Conservative Ministers are converted not only to expansion – they announced the same conversion in 1959 – but to planning as well. Again, I would be the last person to belittle the sacrifice of doctrine and dogma that this involves. Three years ago, when we tabled a Four-Year Plan for Britain, with detailed figures and programmes for production and investment, exports, social expenditure - and, what is more, the means to achieve them -- our proposals were greeted with ribaldry by the Conservatives in the House of Commons. And because they rejected that expansion programme we have had increased unemployment and we have lost two years of increased production which would have enabled us to make an earlier start on these critical and overdue programmes in the fields of education, health, and housing.

In this hall, Sir Alec rightly expressed concern about the steel dispute. I share that concern. He was right to repeat that in every industrial argument there is a third party – the public interest. What he forgot to say was that the depression caused by the Government's stop-go policy in the past three years meant the loss of 11 million tons of steel production, equivalent to the closure of the Abbey Works not for four or five weeks but for four years.

Now we have had a boom which has lasted for less than a year, and already not only the pundits of the financial press and the Bourbons of the economic establishment but serious-minded industrialists are asking how long this one will last. When will it be necessary to apply the brakes? Can the boom hold out till the election comes to save them? Sir Alec's appointment of Mr

Selwyn Lloyd is a timely reminder – the skeleton has returned to the feast.

Now we are asked – as I was on television last week – how are you going to get the sustained increase in production that we need. This is a fair question: it demands a straight answer.

THE PROBLEM OF MAINTAINING EXPANSION
(1) SHORT-TERM

First, we have to distinguish between short-run measures and those of a more long-run character. In the short run, the problem is to steer the existing election boom away from the kind of crisis which so many economic experts now predict later this year, or in early 1965, into a steady and purposive expansion. In the long term, the problem is to create those structural changes in production which are needed to strengthen the economy. This means, above all, achieving the purposive development of those industries we need for increased exports and, wherever it is economic to do so, for substituting home manufactures for imports. It is, too, to repair gaps in the economy, both in terms of physical capital investment and in the numbers and range of trained, skilled workers, so that we do not have to restrain production through shortage either of plant or of skilled craftsmen and technicians.

Let me deal with the short run first: how to stop this present boomlet grinding to a halt.

There are two built-in weaknesses in every Tory period of expansion. The first is the effect of the boom on our balance of payments, that is on both exports and imports. The second is the problem of incomes and inflation. The danger signals are already beginning to flash in respect of both.

So far as the balance of payments is concerned, while exports have increased reasonably well (though considerably less than most of our industrial rivals'), imports are now beginning to turn up much more sharply than exports. The nation may well have to pay a further price for the Government's election gamble. That price rises every month they cling to office, without authority and without policy.

Let me be frank. It is now too late to make the structural changes necessary to restore the balance between exports and imports in time to affect this year's balance of payments, apart from measures to prevent an inflationary increase in prices.

If balance of payments difficulties arise in the next few months we must meet them – as the Government has always said they must be met – by using reserves. The reserves are, in fact, no higher after twelve and a half years of Conservative rule than they were when we left office, only six years after the war. But we should not be afraid to use them, nor, in an emergency, to use our very substantial drawing rights under the International Monetary Fund, to say nothing of other sources which can be mobilized in case of need.

Further, and above that, if necessary, and recognizing that our opponents will have bequeathed us no instrument capable of acting on our balance of payments other than purely monetary weapons, we must be prepared until our defences can be strengthened in other ways to use short-term interest rates to stanch any flow of short-term capital so as to safeguard our sterling area reserves. But in saying this I make one essential condition. If this weapon had to be used as a means of operating on hot money, we should not – as in 1960 and 1961 (and of course 1956–7) – force on the nation a structure of high long-term rates with all that means for investment. And we should take special care by the use of the two-tier interest-rate structure we have proposed to ensure that local authorities get capital for housing, at rates which represent the power of the Government to borrow.

The other threat to the present boom is the danger of inflation through incomes rising faster than productivity. It is a striking commentary on the nature of the new Tory planning that almost before the boom gets under way, with half the country still under-employed, we are talking about pressing on the inflationary ceiling, shortages of skilled workers, and an incomes crisis.

The Labour Party has always stood for an incomes policy based on rising production. I remember clear and firm statements in 1957 and in the crisis of 1961. At the Transport and General Workers' Conference in Scarborough last July, I called for a national and fair incomes policy, related to national productivity against a background of expanding production. At the Labour Party Conference in Scarborough, in October, we adopted by a huge majority a policy of planned growth of incomes, the need for which was recognized by every trade-union leader who came to the rostrum.

We have the right to ask for this policy because we are willing to create the conditions in which it can be established – conditions applying to all incomes, not excluding rents; because we realize the essential unity of social policy and incomes strategy; because we come to the two sides of industry with clean hands with no responsibility for the faith-breaking interference with collective bargaining and industrial conciliation and arbitration that were involved in Mr Selwyn Lloyd's pay pause.

And we can make the national appeal that is needed because, for us, an incomes policy is the condition of sustained growth and because a pledge of sustained growth is a condition of that policy. In the past twelve years, the Conservatives have repeatedly sought to impose a pay freeze because a stagnant economy, indeed an economy forcibly prevented from expanding, could not pay higher wages without inflation.

And let us be clear about this. No policy for incomes is a starter unless we deal with the problem of administered prices. This isn't going to be solved by price war between supermarkets and small traders in the High Street, which at best might reduce the cost of living over a period by a point – 1 per cent. The real problem is the practice recently condemned by Lord Robens of manufacturers who greet a small increase in their wage costs by an utterly disproportionate increase in their selling price. Some of these characters are bleeding industry white. The *Financial Times*, last Wednesday, produced a devastating report, showing that large sections of the engineering industry are demanding price increases of $4\frac{1}{2}$ to 5 per cent, over twice the increase in costs which can be attributed to the recent wage settlement – the excuse for the increases.

THE PROBLEM OF MAINTAINING EXPANSION
(2) LONG-TERM

Now I come to the more important long-term measures that will be needed.

Our weakness lies in the fact that in every crisis of the past few years we heaved a sigh of relief once the run on sterling had been dealt with by borrowing and perhaps interest rate policy, and failed to realize that that was the time to strengthen the economy which would inevitably stop the *next* period of expansion from ending in crisis. You may not be able to mend a leaky roof in a storm but you are a fool if you do not take urgent action as soon as the storm ends to see that it does not leak next time.

The one lesson of the past few years is that you won't make sterling strong by making the economy weak. We condemned attempts to solve our export-import problem by holding production down below the level of our industrial capacity. The key to a strong pound lies not in Britain's finances but in the nation's industry. Finance must be the index, not the determinant, of economic strength.

So the urgent need is to make these structural changes in British industry that will help us to strengthen our export-import relationship and, at the same time, to repair those gaps in the economy – whether of capital equipment or of skilled manpower – which are such a serious limiting factor to continued expansion. Because this is the way to ensure that future expansion does not plunge us into crisis.

On exports: first, markets. There is urgent need to improve facilities and help for small exporters, particularly on a group basis. And the Board of Trade really will have to concern itself more about the uneven quality of after-sales servicing in export markets. The other important need is to set up a Commonwealth Trade Council. We have one for dollar areas, one for Europe. We need one for the Commonwealth, long neglected by Government and wide sectors of industry alike.

On incentives: we have an open mind on proposals for the value-added or turnover tax. We were the first to suggest this in the House of Commons in the summer crisis of 1961. But we should also want to use the tax system vigorously to encourage improved productivity among those industries or parts of industries who have it in their power to increase exports, or to save imports.

A speedier write-off for plant – again, we were the first to suggest the idea which the Chancellor seized on last year – or the use of special investment allowances would be two means of selective encouragement. Year by year, we have moved Finance Bill amendments providing for special tax help in this way. It might or might not be possible to identify individual firms who should be encouraged to expand production because there is a ready market for their goods overseas, particularly in the field of developmental capital for Commonwealth and other countries. But even if it were difficult to identify firms, in any case, it would be possible to identify industries and we should be quite ruthless in discrimination. For industries producing tractors, heavy electrical equipment, or chemical plant, for example, have a much bigger role to play in exports than firms producing shopfitting equipment for the home market.

There is another technique requiring urgent consideration. The prime need of industry is for modernization. We are being left behind each year by the United States, by Germany, by the U.S.S.R., even by France, in the pace of modernization, particularly with automative equipment. We are becoming desperately vulnerable. I suggest, therefore, that just as we once gave special tax encouragement to fuel-saving equipment we should give a decisive investment allowance on a speedy rate of write-off, in respect of all expenditure, particularly named types of automative equipment – at any rate in manufacturing industry. I am not particularly keen to provide Exchequer assistance for the computerization of betting shops, or roulette establishments. But, in essential manufacturing, we need an urgent breakthrough.

I would particularly stress the need to develop import-saving industries. This should be tackled with at least the same urgency as the exports drive. I have always had doubts about Neddy's import and export estimates. But one thing is sure. The safest way to expand production without fear of an overseas trade crisis is to be sure that those products which swell our import bill at times of expansion are, as far as technically possible, produced in this country. I am appalled at the big increase in machinery and semi-finished manufactures that have come into this country in the past few years. I cannot believe that British industry, with appropriate stimulus and help, cannot produce a lot more of these things on a competitive basis. I am not thinking in protectionist terms. I am thinking in terms of help with research and with financing the necessary expansion.

If I were President of the Board of Trade, I should sit down and work out in detail from the Trade Returns all those imports which rise sharply when production increases. Then each would be examined to see whether we could, economically and competitively, find means of producing them in our own factories. The next job would be to discuss with industry, providing Research and Development contracts where necessary, the prospect of developing home-produced substitutes. This would be one of the priority tasks of our new economic planning machinery.

After all, we have had experience of this. After the war, we found we were consuming a great deal more carbon black, used for tyres and other industries. So we got an American firm to establish a factory in the north-west – and saved ourselves foreign exchange. We were importing vast quantities of sulphur, but following a Board of Trade decision, and with considerable Treasury help (all paid back with interest), we established a highly successful and competitive sulphuric acid plant based on indigenous anhydrite.

There are many chemical intermediate products which today we unnecessarily import, and there are many machine tools required for some of our expanding industries. A little has been done, but I should like to see, in addition to tax incentives, Government research and development contracts to provide British equivalents of some of these imports. And success here will be likely to lead to a development of successful export industries.

The other instrument we shall use is the creation of new publicly owned industries based on science. At Scarborough, I referred to the vast and costly research and development contracts which the Government had placed in the past few years for missiles and military aircraft, in many cases hundreds of millions of pounds spent on weapons which never got off the drawing board. What we want to see is research and development contracts aimed at giving us a new breakthrough in civil industry. Again, as the result of Labour legislation, we have had striking successes based on nationally sponsored scientific research, such as the Hovercraft, the Atlas computer and a new breakthrough in fuel cells.

What we now propose is that this sponsored research, to be carried out by Government research institutions, private industry, and C.A.T.s and technological departments of universities, should be sharply stepped up. This is why we have proposed in the House of Commons the creation of a Ministry of Technology to expand civil research and make it more purposive.

But we have asserted that where new industries develop, as a result of community-sponsored research, the community should have an appropriate share of the profits and the control. In some cases, this would mean State-owned industries – and because they were State-owned, we should be able to locate them in areas where work is needed, without all the paraphernalia of cajolery and bribery that is needed with some private enterprises. But others will be joint ventures between public and private ownership, and yet others will be based on licences granted on a royalty or profit-sharing basis.

To the Prime Minister, speaking here in Swansea, the idea of mobilizing science for the future of Britain conjures up ghastly nightmares of 1984, and pink beer. What he should be concerned about is the fact that during the past decade more than 1,100 of our most highly qualified scientists – those with Ph.D.s – and countless other highly qualified engineers and scientists have left these shores, gone abroad, simply because a Conservative-organized country cannot provide them with an adequate outlet for their talents or adequate status and prospects.

Instead of incantations about modernization, he should have told us what his policy is to stop this brain drain and to give science and technology their full place in the planning of Britain's future. Because this is one export which will fall sharply under a Labour Government, the export of British scientists.

Of course, I know that when we talk about science and automation and research and development contracts there are timid Victorians who see in all this a direct threat to our traditional freedoms, including freedom of research. But was National Research Development Corporation's work in sponsoring Hovercraft and the digital computers a derogation of freedom?

DEVELOPMENT AREAS AND DEVELOPMENT INDUSTRIES

At Scarborough, I emphasized the role of science and technology in helping our older industrial areas to make a new breakthrough. Apart from the conscious location of new science-based industries in these areas, I believe we should deliberately aim to steer research contracts to university technological departments and to C.A.T.s in development areas. The research itself would provide work, especially where it involves sub-contracts to local firms. But as research projects develop into new industries, these would come to be located around the research centre. For I would like to see our universities in our industrial areas, and the new ones, which we hope will be located more and more in industrial areas, rather than in cathedral cities, to become the spearhead of our new industrial regeneration. The cross-fertilization of laboratory and workshop will yield a harvest of which we, so far, have no conception.

I believe that there are some industries which will have to be rapidly expanded. I mentioned at Scarborough chemical engineering and chemical plant manufacture which we shall need to expand on a tremendous scale if we are going to get all the orders that are open to us in East-West trade and in Commonwealth development. Here again, the Government can take the initiative in creating a State-sponsored consortium which could use the spare heavy engineering, shipbuilding, and boilermaking capacity in a number of our older industrial areas,

INVESTMENT IN SKILL

Now I turn to the other great need in planning expansion. This is training our people in the skills that are going to be needed. And before we think of post-school training, we have to give the first priority to improving primary and secondary education. This is why it is so important to replace our ancient and, in many cases, dingy city and town schools by new buildings worthy of our children; this is why we have to reduce the size of classes; this is why we have to abolish segregation at the 11-plus stage.

We have given a great deal of study to the improvements that will be needed in higher education. Three months after the Government accepted the Robbins Report, we have still had no decision about Ministerial responsibility for higher education. The Prime Minister simply has no authority to impose a decision on the two senior wranglers who are disputing the decision.

We do not intend to lavish all our care on the fifteen boys and girls out of a hundred who can hope to get a place in a university.

To make the best of our brilliant scientists is vital, but it is just as important to train our great army of technicians, craftsmen, and skilled workers.

For this we need a new deal in apprenticeship and juvenile training. It is a grave condemnation of our system that today, in the midst of this boom of which we heard so much on Monday, so many of our school leavers have still not found work, so many juveniles are drifting between blind-alley jobs and the employment exchange. In Liverpool, near my constituency, they have had to set up three social clubs to keep the young unemployed off the streets.

We are not training enough skilled workers. Nor shall we if it is left to established methods. While some firms have a splendid and unselfish record, there are others who shirk the duty they owe to their industry and the nation, and rely on poaching skilled labour which they have not trained. This is a glaring example of what the economists call the difference between marginal net private costs and marginal net social costs: what is good for profits is not always good for the nation. In more and more industries, apprenticeships should be not with the firm but with the industry. And, as I have suggested, why not bring the State in as a third party to give status and standing to the apprentice in his period of training? And why not provide for more dynamic tax incentives to encourage apprenticeship training?

But the problem is not only one of young workers. An industrial economy which is dedicated to rapid change will require flexible and generous arrangements for training adult workers whose skill has become redundant through the progress of technology. Winding up the Scarborough debate on the scientific revolution, Dick Crossman, speaking for the Executive, stressed the need for the Government to take responsibility for maintaining the living standards of workers whose jobs are rendered obsolete by technical change. The speed of automation in America is such that, while production increases, each new peak in production is marked by a higher and higher level of unemployment. This is why I said months ago that if there had never been a case for Socialism in all the sixty years' history of this Party the automative revolution would produce an economically unanswerable case in the generation to come. For Socialism for us means humanizing what can so easily become a harsh, even brutal technological revolution. This revolution is coming anyway. Socialism in our new Britain will provide that leavening of humanity we never had in the first Industrial Revolution.

Now, Mr Chairman, before I conclude, I want to say something about what all this means for our future policy.

THE MECHANISM OF ECONOMIC PLANNING

The problems we are facing underline the need for effective economic planning covering industrial policy, financial policy, and the application of science to industry. This is why we have been thinking in terms of a Minister of Economic Planning, under a senior Minister, to ensure that an effective national plan is worked out for production, exports, imports, capital investment, and industrial training and technological research.

What Neddy has begun, this Ministry must carry through to

completion, with effective powers for the job. Meanwhile, the Treasury will have the important task, which recent Chancellors have tragically neglected, both of securing control over Government expenditure, and cutting out the prodigious waste in administration – not least in defence – and in producing an up-to-date streamlined tax system which gets rid of the barnacles and moss which have accumulated everywhere, as well, of course, as the traditional tasks of monetary management and responsibility for sterling.

Jim Callaghan has rightly described the job of the tax system as that of providing not a tranquillizer but an energizer.

You will not expect me tonight to anticipate the Labour Chancellor's first Budget, still less any of his other Budgets. His job will be to ensure that the Budget fits in with a national programme of expanding industry.

I think there are three main tasks:

First, in global terms, the Budget must harmonize, and not conflict, with the Cabinet's decision about the rate of expansion. It must provide the right balance of spur or restraint called for by the state of the economy. It will have to provide in the Budget surplus for some of the capital needed for new investment.

Secondly, selectively, it will have to provide the purposive help in expanding those industries which it is essential to expand, and here it will use the tactics I have mentioned.

But, thirdly, it will be the job of the Chancellor to create a climate of social justice which will enable the Government to ask all in industry to join with us in a spirit of partnership.

POLICY FOR TAXATION

What this means in terms of the attack on tax avoidance and the establishment of an effective capital gains tax Jim Callaghan has outlined many times. For *one* reason for the present high rates of personal taxation is the narrowness of the tax base. If you have not much land, you have to build skyscrapers. If the tax base is artificially narrowed by excluding the profits accruing to individuals through speculative gains, the taxation on the rest of us becomes excessive. At the margin, we should like to see a redistribution of the burden, between company taxation and taxes on the individual, to the benefit of the individual. Within company taxation, we should like to see redistribution of the burden, between the lazy and slothful on the one hand, and the energetic and enterprising on the other, by the methods I have outlined. Within the taxation of profits, we should like to see redistribution as between those profits which are paid out as dividends and those which are ploughed back for new development. I am, and always have been, against a statutory limitation of dividends which creates great inequality between companies and which ossifies the economy. But I am strongly in favour of the return to the pre-1958 system of discriminating sharply between distributed and non-distributed profits. Equally we favour dealing with the tax-leak created by the Overseas Trade Corporation provisions of the 1957 Finance Act, which prevents the reserves from benefiting from overseas earnings.

And parallel with justice in the fiscal field there must be fairness within the field of social security. The Conservatives for the past few years have, in times of crisis, increased stamp contributions which bear most heavily on those whose needs are greatest and whose incomes are lowest. In crisis after crisis, they have placed fresh burdens on the sick – the individual prescription charge in 1956, the double prescription charge in 1961 – burdens which they never think of removing in the halcyon months preceding an election. The principle 'from each according to his means, to each according to his needs' is not only a cardinal article of Socialist faith, it is an essential element in the system of social justice which alone can make possible individual restraint and an all-out national effort for increased production.

POLICY FOR INDUSTRY

Equally relevant are our policies in the industrial field: for example, our policy for the public ownership of the steel industry; for in a world based on metal, we cannot leave the vital decisions in this industry, nor questions affecting its efficiency, to be decided by reference to profit as opposed to the national interest.

Again, you cannot plan for expansion if your transport system is to be decided on narrow book-keeping and accountancy considerations. The Government claim to accept planning, yet they have accepted the Beeching Report without any reference to Neddy, without consideration of how N.E.D.C. expansion affects rail traffic and the need for railway services: equally, without any thought of how transport cuts will affect expansion. They talk of bringing industry to Wales and Scotland and the North and then cut out the rail services that will be needed. We have demanded an integrated national transport plan, coordination between rail and road, and the allocation of traffics between them.

It is a problem, too, of dealing with monopolies. The Government pathetically believe that they have solved all our problems by proposing to abolish resale price maintenance and issuing a White Paper about monopolies. All they will succeed in doing by their Bill on resale price maintenance is to repeal the price fixers' charter which they themselves introduced – and which we voted against – in 1956. All they will do on monopolies is to speed the work of the Monopolies Commission by scrapping the brakes which they imposed. If it is a dynamic policy for monopolies which they seek, let them turn to *Signposts for the Sixties* with the powers we propose over mergers, the power to inquire, the power, where necessary, to veto, the power to control.

There is one other industrial problem I must refer to: the load on the building industry. All these vast programmes, however necessary, for houses, schools, universities, hospitals, factories, will strain to the limit and beyond the existing resources of the industry, and its material suppliers. The Government has belatedly recognized the need for new methods of non-traditional building, prefabrication, factory methods, and the rest. This is urgent. But, even so, there will be overloading, and I say quite frankly that we shall not hesitate, in any area where essential programmes are in danger of being crowded out or delayed, to hold back the starting dates of less essential building such as offices built for speculative letting and other forms of luxury building.

Controls, the Tories will say. Yes, you have controls today every time the Ministry of Education cuts out of a local education authority's building programme a new school required to replace some dingy Victorian ancient monument masquerading as an educational establishment. If controls and priorities there must be, let them favour the essential against the inessential.

REGIONAL DEVELOPMENT

The other field of policy and administration in which vast changes will have to be made is in the field of regional development. Jim Callaghan tonight has dealt with problems of bringing industry to the neglected areas of Wales and the west, Scotland and the north. In the years of Labour Government we brought new hope to areas which had been written off in those pre-war Tory years. It will be our task to complete the job that we then began.

But regional development is not a question of industrial location only. The real development we want to see is social development, or urban renewal and urban regeneration, of giving a face-lift to some of our old industrial areas.

This is going to mean effective machinery for deciding land use, and this cannot be achieved – nor can our housing problem be solved – without Labour's plans for public ownership of urban building land. It will mean effective regional planning machinery embracing all the main departments of Government and a real willingness on the part of Whitehall to delegate authority. It will mean a tough line with vested interests, not least in the local authority world. We shall not get the development and regeneration we need unless everyone is prepared to look beyond their own parish and local government boundaries – this includes some Labour-controlled local authorities as well as others. In some parts of the country, we shall have to have planned development machinery on a scale not far short of the Tennessee Valley Authority.

We shall make this task of building a new Britain an exciting one. Our first job is to convince people that it can be done. One of the worst things about the last twelve years has been the defeatism we have become accustomed to accept as normal. That defeatism will vanish with the advent of a Labour Government. For what we offer is an exciting programme calling forth all the finest qualities of our people: their energy, their skill, their tenacity, and their spirit of adventure. We must put behind us the idea that the world owes us a living and that we can muddle on in an amateurish way. Our problem of getting off the ground, of overcoming the forces of inertia, is a problem familiar to the pioneers of space travel. We must develop more thrust. The Tory Party, by its very nature, is incapable of providing this thrust. A Labour Government will provide it. That is how we shall build our new Britain together.

3   A First-class Nation

A speech made at the Usher Hall, Edinburgh, on Saturday, 21 March 1964

... Since 1955 we have seen the Japanese increase their production $3\frac{1}{2}$ times as fast as ours, the Russians $2\frac{1}{2}$ times, the Germans and Italians more than twice, France more than $1\frac{1}{2}$ times. We have been lagging behind. Over twelve years ago, when Labour went out of office, Britain was at the top of Europe's industrial league, and over the twelve years since then we have seen other nations supplant us in our position close to the top of the industrial power league. In steel twelve years ago we led Western Europe, and we were third in the world. Now we have been overtaken by both Germany and Japan – we're down to fifth. British shipbuilding led the world not very long ago – now it leads only on the poster-hoardings. Sir Alec talks of exports; our share in the total world trade in manufactured exports has fallen from 21 to 14.7 per cent in twelve years.

Sir Alec, whose myopic utterances place all the blame on wages, seems not to know that under his Government, for the first time since the days of the early Tudors, German workers take home wages greater than ours, and work fewer hours. For the first time in modern history the Germans are now earning more than our people are; twelve years ago they were lagging behind us by a third. If the trends of the last twelve years continue the Japanese will catch us up by the middle seventies, and by this time the Germans will be twice as powerful economically as we are.

These are not just my thoughts. Let me quote from the *Daily Mail*, who, apart from the euphoria with which they are afflicted as each election draws near, have – in the era of objectivity which besets them between elections – a regard for hard-hitting blunt truths.

The editorial I am going to quote appeared on 13 March 1961, just three years ago, even before Mr Selwyn Lloyd's cataclysmic lurch into economic restrictionism four months later. This *Mail* article quoted and agreed with a statement that 'assuming present trends continue, by 1970 the Germans will be 32 per cent and the French 5 per cent better off than the British, and by 1980 even the Italians will have drawn level.' The *Mail* went on to quote this: 'by the fourth quarter of the twentieth century we shall have so declined as to be among the less advanced countries of Western Europe – unless of course we do better than we have been doing.' It goes on: 'What is the reason? Fundamentally Britain is still one of the finest investments in the world. But for several years we have not been spending enough on modernizing our plant. Germany and France have, and they are reaping the rewards.'

The *Mail* was right. And what they said then – they're not telling this story today of course as we're too near an election – is still true of twelve years of Tory rule.

I don't deny that some have made lush profits under Conservative rule, that finance has flourished even if industry has suffered, that the money-makers have thriven while those who earn money have done less well, that the conspicuous affluence of a few has reached undreamed-of heights. We don't deny this, we have not denied the undoubted rise in living standards: because this has occurred in every industrial country, and a good deal more slowly here in Britain than in most other countries. What we assert is that the industrial engine of our nation's greatness is underpowered, is not developing its full power, and is compelled for too long to idle on two or at best three cylinders.

Because, you see, the Conservatives have really given up hope. They are reconciled to second-class industrial status because the one avenue of escape on which they placed total reliance failed them. For a year and a half they maintained that there was no future for Britain except as part of a wider European industrial complex. Britain – the Tories were told at their 1962 Conference, less than eighteen months ago – Britain is nothing without Europe. We had the undignified spectacle of Tory Ministers on the Llandudno promenade twisting the arms of every delegate along telling them to vote 'yes'; 'yes' to going into Europe on Mr Heath's terms.

And to a nation watching on television, the then Prime Minister said – and this is only eighteen months ago – 'If we were not in Europe', he said, 'our influence would begin to decline, and with the decline of our influence in Europe we should lose our influence in the world outside. . . . Supposing we aren't in it. Supposing we stand outside. Of course we shall go on, but we shall be relatively weak and we shan't find the true strength that we have, and ought to have. We shall not be able to exercise it in a world of giants.' That was a Tory leader, the then Prime Minister, the whole of whose economic, financial, foreign, and even defence policies had been based on the assumption that somehow we were going to get into the European Common Market.

I have news for the Conservative leaders. We didn't get into Europe. But their arguments – if they were correct in saying that we must turn our backs on the Commonwealth in seeking entry regardless of the terms, regardless of the conditions; if all that were true, then on their arguments our failure to get in would mean that we should be condemned to an inexorable decline, to second-class, and ultimately to third-class, status.

The Labour Party, Mr Chairman, reject this grovelling, this defeatist doctrine of humiliating impotence. We reject the dismal tones of friends abroad who say that we have lost our way in the world, that our flame is burning low, that we have nothing to offer except the memories and nostalgia of a faded imperial grandeur, or the feudal glories of our tourist attractions, or our ancient monuments in Scotland – and in the Cabinet. We think we have more to offer.

We reject this doctrine, as we reject the failure to develop vital industries in which not long ago we led the world – our failure to develop the new industries where our science and technology have fitted us to lead, but where we have quitted the field without a struggle.

One major factor in our economic weakness is our growing dependence on imports for goods that we should be making ourselves in this country – goods we are perfectly capable of making, economically, efficiently, without protectionist devices. I am not suggesting any policy of economic autarky. But there are many imported goods which we could be producing if the Government were showing leadership, and if industry were showing more enterprise.

Compared with ten years ago, we are now importing every year something like £1,000 millions more of manufactured goods, some of them finished consumer goods, television sets, cars, clothing, footwear, some of them machinery which we ought to be able to make in this country for ourselves and be exporting to the whole world: as well as some semi-finished manufactures, some chemicals. I cannot believe that we could not be producing a high proportion of all this import total ourselves, on an economic basis, if the right energy and drive had been shown. Industry after industry, as year succeeds year, turns over from being a major exporter to being a net importer.

It's not that we lack the inventors and the innovators. Britain pioneered jet aircraft. Yet our airlines are dependent on foreign planes – only in engines do we still lead – our Navy has to go to the U.S. for the new aircraft it needs. And to the U.S. for Army and Navy helicopters too: a week or two ago we had the Minister of Defence in the House of Commons not even presenting the facts and the figures because he was afraid of having to confess that we had to go cap-in-hand to America for essential military and naval aircraft; whether to import them or to build them here on the basis of foreign know-how on a royalty basis. This is humiliating.

British science made atomic energy possible. Yet with all our great maritime tradition we lag behind with nuclear propulsion for merchant shipping. The nuclear submarine has fallen behind in its programme, and its designated commander has been given another command.

In maritime nuclear propulsion we are now depending on the Belgians, who came into the nuclear field a long time after we did. Lord Hailsham's own pet project has been dropped. The Government has failed. Industry has not come through, and now, to quote the Science Correspondent of the *Sunday Times*, a fortnight ago, 'A British-made nuclear ship is as far away as ever although development costs for its marine reactor have already soared to £3,000,000. The £3 millions was spent before the end of last year, and by the end of the research period the figure is expected to rise to at least £5 millions and still nothing to show for it.'

Not long ago our machine-tools industry led the world. Now we are major importers of some of the most important types. We have let the world pass us by, and this is not unconnected with the fact that a Government report not long ago showed that in that vast industry we had only a handful of graduate engineers engaged on research.

Or, again, take chemicals, where our scientists and chemical research workers are as good as any in the world, but where in major fields enterprise is sluggish. In certain branches of chemical engineering, too, we lack the know-how and the organization to turn chemical discoveries made in this country into great engineering industries, and we have to go abroad to get other engineers to turn our inventions into new industrial developments. If you take chemical products since 1953, our exports of chemicals have increased by 50 per cent and our imports have quadrupled. Couldn't we have done more of that ourselves on a competitive basis?

Or take computers, where at the end of the war we held an unrivalled position. We have, in fact, had one significant breakthrough – the Atlas computer, which was State-sponsored. The research began in Manchester University, the development work was taken over by the National Research Development Corporation, a State enterprise which the Labour Government set up in 1948, and as a result we have had this great breakthrough with the Atlas computer being exported to the highly transistorized, computerized, United States of America. But for the rest, we have seen the Americans ride rough-shod over our computer achievements. Other countries have caught us up and left us behind in their use. In Sweden, for every million workers in the country in their manufacturing industries (excluding agricultural workers) at the end of last year 47 computers had been installed or were on order; so had Switzerland. Germany had 27, France had 26, and Britain had 17. We had 750 machines here (nearly one third of them imported from abroad) compared with about 12,000 in the United States.

Is Sir Alec really content to see us falling behind in these industrial fields.

Now I know what he will say – he'll say that I am selling Britain short. But it is not our words that are doing that. It is their actions – and their inaction, their drift, their failure over twelve years to strengthen the industrial power in this country.

And as our relative industrial power has declined, it has been our great producing areas such as Scotland and Wales and north-east England that have suffered, with unemployment, emigration and depopulation.

Mr Chairman, we reject this doctrine of inevitable second-class status, of inevitable decline, of increasing dependence. We have put forward a dynamic, purposeful alternative that can enable Britain to regain her rightful place in the world, and her rightful influence. Everyone of us knows that in this divided, distracted world, torn apart not only by the east–west conflict, but by the north–south conflict, by racial conflict and suspicion – and the problems of poverty and hunger – everyone of us who travels abroad knows that the world is looking to Britain for a lead, that no one else can give it. But you won't give that lead if you are skirting on the dangers of economic crisis.

What then needs to be done?

First of all we have got to have planning for expansion, not just one year in every four, but steady purposive planning year in and year out. And by planning we don't mean the publication of academic statistics and blueprints, but plans and priorities – planning with teeth.

Neddy was, and I concede this – I conceded this the day it was announced – Neddy was a big step forward for a Conservative Party which has always rejected the very doctrine of planning or any interference with the free market.

I remember in 1961, just three years ago, we presented in the House of Commons a Four-Year Plan for Britain, a plan for increased production for increased exports, a plan to take care of the imports that would follow, or in some cases precede the increased production, a plan for social expenditure and social development, and housing. When that plan was presented in the House of Commons on 7 February 1961, the Tories guffawed.

They were against planning; yet only four months later, in the agonies of the 1961 crisis, Mr Selwyn Lloyd, then Chancellor, announced that the Tories accepted planning and were setting up the National Economic Development Council. Eighteen months after that we got the figures from Neddy and they were very close indeed to the figures that we ourselves had tabled in those early months of 1961.

But we had lost a couple of years. When the Tories say how are you going to pay for all those housing plans, and how are you going to pay for all this education, let us remind them of the years when we failed to increase production in this country. If Labour's Four-Year Plan had been put into effect in the early months of 1961, we would by this time have been producing something like £3,000 millions worth more of goods and services in this country. Could not some part of that £3,000 millions have been devoted to clearing up the back-log in housing and schools and the hospital programme and the rest? The Chancellor would have been getting £1,000 millions more in increased tax revenue, without raising a single rate of tax.

But, you know, now that we have got from the Tories the N.E.D.C. plan in its broad outlines, this isn't enough; we need more than paper plans. Last week the F.B.I. rejected any plans to deal with prices, and profits and dividends. Neddy's writ doesn't run among the top brass of British industry, and as long as that is true there is no hope of any Tory plan.

But secondly, Mr Chairman, planning means industrial priorities and it means social priorities. And this is what Tory ideology rejects.

A free market for the land speculator – this is something Sir Alec demands with unaccustomed passion. He doesn't get passionate about many things, but on television two or three weeks ago, when asked what his policy for interest rates for housing was, he got into a tremendous passion about the need to have a free market in land. It was the wrong answer to the wrong question, but at any rate we saw his sincerity blazing through in that particular hour.

So far from believing in planning, they believe in a free market for profits, for dividends, for tax-free capital gains. They believe in freedom for the speculative property developer to build vast office blocks, sucking in their employees against a background of depopulation in the north and in the west.

But at the same time don't let them tell you they don't believe in controls. Remember their tighter restriction on new schools over the past twelve years for instance; the tighter restrictions on council house building and on advance factories – until the election drew near. Sir Alec tells you that a Labour Government will mean tying you hand and foot in the toils of bureaucracy. But we get controls from the Tories all the time – the wrong ones, because the distortion of Tory economic ideology means that whatsoever things are profitable, whatsoever things give someone an uncovenanted capital gain – however inessential they may be from the social point of view – those things are allowed and encouraged, and capital can be found for them. But whatsoever things are socially necessary, whatsoever developments are needed to clear the slums that we saw this morning here in Edinburgh, whatsoever measures are needed to build the schools and the hospitals and the advance factories, these are subject to the tight-fisted control of Her Majesty's Treasury, of the Ministry of Housing and Local Government, and of St Andrew's House, here in Edinburgh.

We say, and we are quite frank about this: we reject their conception of control, but if it is necessary to hold back less essential building projects in the private sector – however profitable – in order to give the go-ahead to essential schemes of industrial or social construction, we shall not hesitate to apply the priorities that are necessary.

And in our order of priorities replacement of the slum areas we saw this morning, the building of new factories to create jobs, the schools to give millions of kids a better chance in life than they look like getting under the Tories: these are of higher priority than the building of office blocks.

Because, you see, the essence of Tory policy is abdication – abdication of responsibility for the nation's economic well-being. They feel it is right to leave all the vital decisions to be taken, not by Ministers responsible to Parliament, not by the elected representatives of the people, but by irresponsible (in the constitutional sense of the word irresponsible) take-over bidders and speculators and financiers. All these people by their decisions are applying controls all the time.

If they hog a substantial proportion of the nation's economic resources for their developments there is nothing left over for the schools and the housing and the hospitals and the factories and the rest. Controls are being applied – they are being applied by Mr Clore and his friends, not by a Government responsible in the House of Commons.

The Tories will fight to the death to prevent the British people from owning their own steel industry. But when a private take-over bidder motivated not by social purpose but by private gain comes along, or when some powerful American interest comes along to bid for some vital British concern, they stand aside, they encourage this, they say it is good. You mustn't control your own steel industry, but it's all right for an American Corporation to come along and take over some vital British firm. Because, you see, when that happens fortunes are made for a privileged few because of the rise in share values that results.

I can recall a case not very long ago, under this Government, when in a few minutes one sunny Friday morning any stockholder – owning a few thousand pounds' worth of stock affected by an American take-over – made more money tax-free in ten minutes than an engine driver, or a shipyard worker, or a miner could make in a whole lifetime of work for the community.

This is their sense of values, and a Conservative Chancellor blessed the transaction with all his heart, and 300 Tory M.P.s tramped through the Lobby and supported it.

And thirdly, Mr Chairman, we believe that the regeneration of British industry means, as we have said time and time again, the purposive application of science to Britain's industry. We need more scientists, we need more technologists, we need more engineers, we need much greater encouragement to those among us who are capable of innovation, of technical skill for scientific research – and the application of all these things to industry.

British scientists, I believe, lead the world when we can keep them in this country. Where we so often fall behind is in the application of the results of their research to industrial processes.

When the brain drain problem hit the headlines, we had from Lord Hailsham, as he then was – now Mr Hogg – the crassest remark we have ever had from that particular Rt Hon. gentleman. He said 'they were leaving this country and going to America because of the deficiencies of the American educational system.' He never thought of asking whether it wasn't because of the deficiences of the British industrial system or of the British Government's management of research and technology, in that it did not give the status, the prospects, and the dignity, and the opportunities that these highly trained scientists and technologists should have.

And this, Mr Chairman, is why we, in our plans, give priority to the establishment of a Ministry of Technology to put some drive behind the industrial applications of science.

And fourthly, this programme cannot succeed unless we mobilize all our people, and the new generation now at school, on the basis of equality of opportunity, and of a chance in life that their parents never had. A vast expansion in teaching facilities is needed, and just as important as expanding our universities is the need to improve facilities for industrial training, for apprenticeships, for further education.

The Tories, after voting us down year after year on programmes for university expansion, rushed at the Robbins Report last October to give them the image of modernization and of progressive thought. We believe that the Robbins Report in its emphasis on higher education is right. We believe that it is a condemnation of the years of Tory government that these steps weren't taken in time. We believe that Robbins will probably be shown to have underestimated, not overstated, the problem, because I don't think Robbins has made enough allowance for the boys and girls from working-class homes who because of the deficiencies in our educational system don't even get to the point of applying to the universities.

As one of our great scientists, Professor Blackett, said in his Guildhall lecture, not long ago, 'the problem is that so many bright boys and girls don't get into universities, not because they knock and are turned away. They don't even knock.'

I have just had the privilege of addressing the annual gathering of the Heads of Technical Colleges in Britain, and I could see in what I was told there that no area of education is more neglected today than that of further education in technical colleges, which provide an education for so many who have missed opportunities through no fault of their own, because of the working of the present system.

Fifthly: we need a true industrial partnership in this country, based on effort and reasonable restraint.

In the agonies of this year, as the economic pattern and election timing seem to be getting out of gear with one another, the Tories are turning more and more to an appeal for wages restraint.

Sir Alec, in Glasgow, appealed to me to help, in using the influence he said we had with the unions, to support a Tory Government in wage restraint. No one I think has shown greater courage than the Labour Party in emphasizing, when it has not been popular to do so, the need for an incomes policy in this country.

We did it – yes, when we were the Government; but we were not afraid to cause unpopularity at a difficult time, with the great lead Sir Stafford Cripps gave.

We've done it in Opposition. Hugh Gaitskell and others of us. Last year I chose the occasion of the Conference of the Transport and General Workers' Union to make an appeal for an incomes policy in this country. And we can get an incomes policy, provided it is a true incomes policy, covering profits and dividends, prices and rents, as well as wages and salaries. You can't pass the Rent Act one year, force up rents, add to insecurity, create hardship for millions of families, and then come along and ask for wage restraint. You can't ask for an incomes policy if you first cut production down and then say that having reduced production we will now hold wages down in line with productivity.

You can ask for this policy if production and productivity are rising, you can ask for it if it is intended, if it is envisaged, against the background of a climate of true social justice.

But you don't cut surtax one minute and ask for wage restraint the next. You don't preach sermons about arbitration, if you use your position as a Government, when you are an employer, to tear up solemnly negotiated arbitration agreements, as the present Government did in the autumn of 1961.

We are facing a very difficult industrial situation in more than one direction. But it does not lie in the mouths of the Government to talk about arbitration and the honouring of collective bargaining agreements.

Mr Chairman, we have the right to talk like that, because our hands are clean.

A sixth condition of Britain's industrial regeneration is the use of taxation as an energizer, stimulating the laggard firm, rewarding the efficient, and creating a climate of social justice.

And the seventh point, on which I end, is this. We cannot get the regeneration of British industry, or strength in Britain's economy, unless we get a completely new drive on the subject of the location of industry in the most needy areas.

Hasn't it struck you how totally fantastic is the present economic position in this country? The Tories will do what they can to get the pre-election boom running until the election – whenever that is. But if you ask any economic pundit in the City of London, any City Editor or financial journalist, how he describes the economy today, he will say it is overheated: it's going too fast, we're getting too prosperous, and we'll have to do something about it.

We are now faced with the situation that the election boom is running into difficulties through overheating in London and the south-east, and the industrial Midlands. This at a time when Scotland, north-east England, Merseyside, and parts of Wales and the west, have not yet emerged from the ice age caused by Mr Selwyn Lloyd's freeze imposed after the last election.

They have not merely allowed this two-nation system to develop: they have actually let it worsen since the election so that every time we run into overheating in the south you've got to slam the brakes on, slam the freezer on, or whatever metaphors they like to use at any particular moment, and this at a time when prosperity has barely begun to touch the neglected areas.

In the last election we had the promises. I remember Mr Macmillan's speech in Glasgow and his promise to bring work to the people of Scotland. We had the much trumpeted Local Employment Act in 1960, which has ended as a tinkling cymbal.

In all these Parliamentary battles about Scotland's unemployment problems in the last two to three years, may I pay tribute to the Scottish Group of Labour Members, for the fight they have made. There has been no more coherent, no more effective, and sometimes no more frightening group of Members of Parliament since the days of Parnell and his Irishmen, as led by Willie Ross, George Willis, Jimmy Hoy, Peggy Herbison, and Tom Fraser, who have seized every occasion, and when there wasn't one created it. In season and out, in order and out of order, they've pressed the claims of Scotland – yes, and of other areas too.

But how does the Government think we are going to solve the problem and bring employment to these areas when they have the Beeching Report?

I am not criticizing Dr Beeching. It was a very fine piece of accountancy, of book-keeping, or, if you like, of surgery. But the Government set him the job of surgery without telling him to produce a diagnosis first. Of course, as the election approaches Mr Marples is drawing back a little on the Beeching cuts. But I remember what he said in the debate last April. 'This programme', he said, 'is the first third of the lines to be closed down, the second third will be coming along very soon, when you've got this out of the way.'

How can you plan for expanding production if you don't plan the nation's transport at the same time?

In Scotland, if these proposals go through, you will find development district after development district, and even the scheduled area of Central Scotland itself, affected by rail closures. If these proposals go through you will not have a new town in Scotland which has a railway station of its own. And they talk about planning.

Mr Chairman, we shall not solve this problem unless nationally we get up a head of steam through the measures I have put forward – economic planning, the creation of new industries, and the application of science to industry. But, equally, we won't solve our problems unless we can ensure, by resolute measures of industrial policy, that a fair, and a more than fair, share of that head of steam is diverted into the areas where work is needed.

I don't think you will solve problems by bribes and cajolery and trying to persuade some reluctant industrialist to go here rather than there. I certainly don't believe you'll begin to solve it on the basis of the Government's new proposals for the south-east, which envisage a continuing depopulation of Scotland and the north-west, and the north-east of England.

I believe we are only going to solve this problem now by creating new areas, by regenerating areas of social and economic decline, and by the creation of new industries, many of which will have to be publicly owned.

The Tories will say: Nationalization. But I am not talking in that context about the transfer of industries at present privately owned into public hands. I'm talking about industries private enterprise has neglected to create, and which we shall have to create. And which, having been created, we can – because they will be publicly owned and under public control – site in these areas without the necessity of cajolery, or bribery, or Ministers humiliating themselves by going down on their knees to some industrialist to set up a factory where it is socially necessary that he should do so.

With these means, Mr Chairman, we can achieve the steady increase in production that we need. Production to end poverty in these islands; production to make possible vast programmes of social improvement which were dramatically and tragically underlined for everyone of us who were in those areas of Freer Street and Jamaica Street this morning. The housing conditions we saw this morning were an affront to a civilized nation, and in saying that one does not single out Edinburgh, because we know we shall find them in other cities in Scotland and in England. I know what conditions are like on Merseyside.

But haven't the people who live in these areas, as citizens of this country, the same right to a home and the same right to a chance in life as any of those in favour of whom the scales in this Tory society are so heavily weighted today?

We know of the waiting lists, of the overcrowding, and we saw something of it this morning. All of us as Members of Parliament know of the problems of young couples on local authority housing lists. This is the great tragedy of our time.

Here we are in 1964, in the middle of the great scientific revolution in world history, with science making more progress in the last fifteen years than it has in the last 1,500 years, and yet there are millions of people who have got no bath in their home, no inside lavatory, no internal hot-water system. We saw some of these homes this morning.

It is in the ways I have outlined, not by illusory nuclear posturings, that we shall restore Britain's standing in the world. I believe the world is looking to us for a lead. I believe when the issue is put to the test, this great movement, standing as it now is poised on the very threshold of power, will be true to itself, to the pioneers who created this great movement, and will be true to the nation and the world.

4   Housing and Planning

A speech delivered at the Town Hall, Leeds, on Saturday, 8 February 1964

... In my two speeches in Birmingham and Swansea I have dealt with the kind of new Britain we seek to build and with the economic policy we must follow if we are to build it.

Today, I want to talk a little about the social environment in which we shall be operating. This is an age of the so-called affluent society – walk along the banks of the Aire and the Calder and you will think that this is a Macmillanite slip of the tongue for effluent society.

Modern science, modern technology, modern industry, are capable of producing a nation in which poverty and rank bad living conditions can be outlawed for ever. In two decades the scientists have made more progress than in the past two thousand years. They have made it possible for man to reach out to the moon. Yet in our large industrial towns about one third of the households have no bathrooms and about one quarter have no piped hot water. Nearly half our hospitals survive as ancient monuments, whispering their last carbolic tribute to the age of Queen Victoria. Over half of the primary schools in which the children of the new Britain are being educated were built in the nineteenth century. Twelve years of Tory freedom have failed to produce the replacement rate of our social capital which even keeps pace with the rate of obsolescence. We are going to create a great breakthrough in science and technology – not for further advances in the techniques of thermo-nuclear destruction, but to construct the cities of the future, cities worthy of our people.

This is one of the great challenges to Britain's new government: the regeneration of our older urban – and indeed rural – areas. Let me begin with housing. And before we come to the hundreds of thousands of slums and out-dated properties, let us first recognize the fact of the countless families who have no separate home of any kind. There are the families in London and in other big cities and towns – a growing army of the homeless, in all thousands of families divided, desperate, condemned if they are to find shelter at all to the care of the local authorities; in many cases, compelled to live in ancient Poor Law institutions that should have been blown up years ago. Then you have the families waiting for a house, in many cases living with in-laws, or even with their families divided, husband and wife living apart.

The City of Liverpool alone, which is the housing authority for the majority of my constituents, has forty thousand families on its housing list, and I know of many more who don't even bother to register as they don't think it is worthwhile. And in that same city, there are 80,000 scheduled slums.

The free market in housing has broken down.

The primary housing need in this country is for homes to let. And this is precisely what the Conservatives have failed to provide. The number of council houses built last year, in 1963, was 124,000, 66,000 less than were built when Aneurin Bevan was Housing Minister in 1948, only three years after the end of the war.

We were told that the Rent Act of 1957 would act as a miraculous solvent, that more houses would be built to let, that higher rents would end the queues. Millions of families now know that these Tory promises have proved a cruel delusion. The Rent Act has not only failed to solve the housing problem as its authors promised, but has made it far worse, and caused an upheaval for hundreds of thousands of innocent families and brought far more under the threat of arbitrary eviction.

What, then, has to be done? The first thing is to give the green light to local councils. Too often they have been held back and confined during the years of the stop-go economy and then given an all-clear on the eve of an election.

But this is not all. The local authorities of this country will not be able to build the houses we need, whether for the homeless, those living in overcrowded conditions, the divided families, the young married couples, all those awaiting slum clearance, until two conditions are realized: first, that land must be made available, in adequate amounts and at reasonable prices; second, that the capital needed to finance house building must be provided at reasonable rates of interest.

First, the land. How many local authorities can say that they have the land zoned and allocated and in their possession, for even the minimum number of houses which have to be built. I have a new local authority in my constituency which faces one of the worst housing problems in Britain. Yet, over more than two years, despite prayers, entreaties, letters from the M.P., and some tough exchanges in the House, the Tory Housing Minister failed even to give sanction for acquiring the necessary land. Families went on living in tragic, heart-rending conditions. Finally, a small parcel of land was allocated, and the first totally inadequate housing programme started.

Then that great apostle of modernization, the Member for North-east Leeds,* that recent convert to land nationalization, became Housing Minister. In October 1962 I led a housing deputation to him: the council wanted to plan their housing programme instead of proceeding on a hand-to-mouth basis. Sir Keith was impressed; he promised to consider their request as a matter of urgency. Twelve months later, as he was imaginatively adding more phantom houses to his election target, the council had not even had the courtesy of a reply. There is one urgently needed change in Government arrangements. Planning decisions, decisions about land use, must be vigorously decentralized, and the long costly delays eliminated.

The other urgent problem about land is its cost. For even where the land is available, it is rapidly being priced far beyond any reasonable economic level. Local authorities are finding that land which they had provisionally zoned for rented housing two or three years ago at a price which, even then, was beyond all reason is now increased in value still further.

On Wednesday, the House of Commons learnt of land north of London worth in April last year £250 an acre, for farming. Today, having been scheduled for building, it is selling at £10,000 an acre. In Enfield, the London *Evening Standard* reported only last month, the Council is being asked to pay no less than

*Sir Keith Joseph.

£250,000 for a twelve-acre site which only three years ago was sold for less than £7,500.

This is why the Labour Party is determined to take urban building land into public ownership. When we said this, our plan was denounced by Sir Keith Joseph and other Tories as rank Socialism, unworkable, as a denial of our fundamental liberties. It was only as the election drew near that even Sir Keith followed the example of his colleagues and announced his acceptance of yet another Socialist principle, the public ownership of building land. Little Sir Echo again. And, like most other Tory pre-election conversions, I think this new-found enthusiasm could last just as long as the election and not many days afterwards.

The other urgent need, if the land is to be found, is for more new towns. For ten years, right up to 1961, the Conservatives refused to start a single new town in the whole of England and Wales. New repentance is setting in, yet after a further three years not one new house has been built in any of the areas designated for Merseyside and the west midlands.

So much for land. The other problem is interest rates. The typical council house in 1951 cost £1,400. The same house (or rather the smaller house the Government now considers adequate for ordinary families) today costs over £2,000. But the building cost is only a fraction of the problem. Because of changes in interest rates, the total costs over sixty years are still greater. With the Public Works Loans Board lending at 3 per cent, the 1951 house cost altogether just over £3,000. At today's P.W.L.B. rate of 5¾ per cent, the 1963–4 house costs over £7,000. Thus interest charges, including of course the interest on the higher land prices, add £4,000 to the all-in cost of the house – the equivalent of 25s. a week extra rent.

Why have local authorities and, consequently, ratepayers and tenants been muleted in this way? It is because, for the first few years of the Tory administration, the Government could think of no other way of regulating the economy except by the pre-1914 mechanism of monetary manipulation and excessive interest rates. When this policy failed to bite, they closed the doors of the Public Works Loans Board to most local authorities and forced them on to the market. So they found money harder to get, much more costly to borrow, and essential housing schemes suffered. We condemned this reversion to economic anarchy, and our protests received the authoritative backing of the Radcliffe Committee on Monetary Policy which reported in 1959, before the last Election. Now, of course, on the eve of the 1964 Election, the Government are weaving their way unsteadily back towards the Public Works Loans Board as a means of financing the local authorities.

A Labour Government would revert to Public Works Loans Board financing for essential local authority needs and ensure that that financing will be at a reasonable rate of interest which reflects the power of the Government to borrow.

But in addition to houses to let we have the problem of the many families who wish to buy their own houses. Here again, we have tragic cases of young couples with perhaps a growing family, of families affected through the operation of the Rent Act, or of couples getting married, who are priced out of the market by land racketeering, and who, if they can find land on which to build, or an older house that they wish to buy, are forced to pay excessive mortgage rates because of the Tory monetary policy.

Our land policy will bring land prices down to reasonable levels. It will also unfreeze the substantial areas of land which have been bought by property companies or private individuals as a speculation and which, at the moment, are sterilized in the hope of still further capital gains. Equally, the would-be house owner will be helped by our proposals for mortgages at reasonable interest rates.

At Bury, on Monday, Sir Alec, forgetting his Swansea strictures about class-consciousness, flat-footedly asserted that no one 'who owns a house or wants to own a house can possibly vote Socialist', implying no doubt that no one who pays rent, whether to a private landlord or to a Council housing department, should vote Conservative. We reject this artificial division of our people into Class 1 and Class 2 citizens. We expect that a very substantial proportion of both tenants and owner-occupiers will vote Labour this time, and others, no doubt, will vote Conservative or Liberal. There are thousands of owner-occupiers who have voted Conservative in the past who have learnt their lesson as a result of increased land prices – and hence increased house prices – and the increased mortgage charges which are the direct result of this Government's policies.

But what about the millions of privately owned rented houses in which so many of our people are living? We all enjoy *Coronation Street*, but the Coronation Streets of this country have no baths, and no hot-water systems. Many of them have no internal lavatories.

Let us turn now to the hard facts of people's homes.

Six million of Britain's houses – well over a third of the total – were built when Queen Victoria was on the throne. Nearly 3 million of them are over 100 years old. Yet the Tories have plans to replace only half a million of them. These are the balance of the slum clearance programme which started in 1956.

The local councils estimated in 1960 that besides the recognized slums there are roughly 1½ million houses with a further life of *under* fifteen years. Because of their short expectation of life these houses are ineligible for improvement grants. Yet the Tories have no plans for replacing or even repairing these incipient slums.

There are over 4 million houses with a life of *over* fifteen years which are eligible for improvement grants because they lack essential amenities – baths, hot-water systems, w.c.s.

I am a son of the West Riding. The 1961 Census Report has just been published. It shows that over 300,000 households in the West Riding (a quarter of the total) are still entirely without fixed baths, and over 200,000 (a third of the total) have no hot water. If you take the figures for Barnsley, Dewsbury, Halifax, Sheffield, and, I am sorry to say, Huddersfield, about a third of the households still lack bathrooms and about a quarter lack piped hot water.

The advertisers show us Mrs 1970 in her centrally heated modern home. But millions of British housewifes are still struggling to make do with the housing conditions of Mrs 1870. Unless we greatly increase the pace of replacing and modernizing our outdated stock of houses, yet another generation will be brought up in homes which lack even the elementary amenities of modern life.

The vast majority of the houses lacking baths, hot water, and the other basic amenities are terraced properties owned by private landlords. A government report estimates that 2½ million houses owned by private landlords are eligible for improvement grants in England and Wales alone. Against this figure, private landlords are modernizing only 25,000 houses a year with the help of local authority grants.

At this rate, they will take a 100 years to deal with all these homes.

The plain fact is, as we have long recognized, rented housing is not a proper field for private profit, still less for the odious system under which private companies can buy and sell people's homes for the sake of unearned and uncovenanted capital gains.

This is why, in our policy, we have said that a Labour Government will raise the standard of fitness for our houses. The present standard was fixed in the nineteenth century. We shall replace it by one which reflects modern standards. It will include the provision of a fixed bath or shower, hot water, and an internal lavatory.

Landlords will be required, area by area, to bring their property up to this standard with the help of improvement grants, or sell it to the local authority. If the landlord refuses to do either, the local council will purchase the house compulsorily and improve it. At this stage, the tenant will be given the chance to buy the house if he wishes to.

Very old houses not worth improving up to the new standard will be listed for clearance and will be temporarily improved where they cannot be pulled down in five years.

Now I come to the special problem of Rachmanism. For years, Labour M.P.s produced evidence of the Rachmanite empires in Paddington, south London, and in other towns and cities. For years, Ministers smugly denied the existence of the problem. Last year, newspaper revelations of the operations of Rachman led to a Parliamentary debate where, once again, Sir Keith Joseph and his colleagues rejected evidence we produced and the solution we offered. For years, they have failed to deal with underground housing operators, who fleece their tenants behind a smokescreen of anonymity. When we suggested that local authorities should deal with these racketeers by nailing a requisition notice against the door – from which moment no one could claim rent except the local authority – Sir Keith Joseph was roused to passionate abuse. But once again, as the election grows nearer, we find him introducing a belated Bill giving some of the powers for which we had asked. Meanwhile, decent families have lived in terror of eviction, paying rents they can ill afford, subject even to violence by these racketeers and their hirelings.

Let me repeat: The Labour Government will repeal the 1957 Rent Act, and replace it by a measure providing machinery for a fair settlement of rents as between landlords and tenants.

We shall stop all further decontrol of rents, including the creeping decontrol which occurs every time property changes hands. It is significant that the Conservatives have refused to answer our challenge to them to ask whether, if they are elected, any further rent decontrol will take place. Perhaps one reason is that the Property Council, the powerful group of property owners and developers who exercise such influence in the Conservative Party, have issued a demand that if the Conservatives are elected all rent control should go.

With a Labour Government, not only will there be no further decontrol, but the Rent Act will be repealed. Evictions will stop and tribunals will be set up to settle fair rents.

And we shall give local authorities full powers to step in to deal with the Rachmans and the other housing racketeers.

HOSPITALS

And it is not only a question of homes. Nearly half our hospitals were built in the last century; 45 per cent of them, in fact, before 1891. One in five was built before 1861, when Florence Nightingale was in her prime.

Two or three years ago, a survey was made on hospital care of the aged in Birmingham, and it referred to 'hospitals which should have been blown up, slum property, appalling fire risks, overcrowding, barrack-like buildings, and degrading conditions for patients and staff'. And in twelve years of this Government, in the affluent years of the twentieth century, we have built precisely five new hospitals – not enough to keep pace with the rising population.

Contrast this rate of hospital building with the ever-increasing speed of the revolution in medical science. This century, and particularly the last twenty years, have seen enormous advances in medical science. Operations on the heart and brain are achieving incredible results. Antibiotics have revolutionized treatment of many diseases. But the hospitals in which the surgeons and nurses have to work were built when medical science was in its infancy.

The accommodation into which we put our old people should outrage the nation's conscience. In Britain today, 80,000 old people are in homes – local authority residential welfare accommodation. Of these, over half are in former public assistance institutions, workhouses, whose early disappearance was planned by Aneurin Bevan in 1948 when he was Minister of Health. Sixty per cent of these institutions are over 100 years old, some of them go back 200 years. Recent research suggests that even at the completion of the Government's existing ten-year plan for the development of health and welfare service 14,000 would still be living in ex-workhouses, and this more than a quarter of a century after Labour had said that workhouses must go.

SCHOOLS

From our older citizens, I turn to the youngest.

The pattern of ancient monuments is as true of our schools as it is of institutional accommodation. Half of our primary schools, 55 per cent in fact, are still using premises designed in the Victorian era. Sixty per cent of these schools have no separate dining-room for children to have school dinners. Forty-three per cent of primary schools have no inside lavatories: They are all in the yard outside. Half have no playing fields and more than half no assembly hall. Forty per cent have no staff room. Nothing is as important as this for giving staff a breathing space away from the children, to prepare lessons and to mix with other staff. No wonder so many young staff find teaching lonely and depressing, especially when they are faced with classes of over forty. No wonder there's a problem in recruitment of teachers.

One in five secondary modern schools were built last century and two in five before 1918. The Newsom Report said that these schools were 'seriously deficient'.

Only 38 per cent of secondary modern schools have adequate specialist accommodation for science. Only a quarter have a proper library. The Newsom report says 'often enough the only facilities for experiments involving the use of gas, electricity, or water are at the teacher's bench.'

Only one in three, says Newson, have 'adequate' playing fields.

Grammar schools are affected too. Three in ten are using premises built last century. One in five has no separate dining-room or gymnasium.

In 1961, the Science Masters' Association conducted a survey which showed that 26 per cent of independent schools had laboratories which came up to the standard adopted by the 'Industrial Fund' which collects tax-free donations from big business in order to distribute funds to public schools. Only 1 per cent of local authority grammar schools had laboratories up to this standard.

Stung by the approach of the Election and the anger aroused by the Newsom Report, the Government have now announced a last-minute increase in new school building. We have had these promises before. The 1959 pledge was not kept in real terms of bricks and mortar. The plain fact is that Conservative pre-election repentance survives an election result by only a few months. The inexorable restrictions of the stop-go economy operate with redoubled ferocity against social investment. We are, even today, suffering under the restrictions in the modern school building programme imposed during Mr Selwyn Lloyd's 1961 crisis.

When we talk about holding back the starting date of less essential building to allow a priority social and industrial programme a clear right of way, the Conservatives invoke the old cry of 'controls'. What they will not admit is that this

Government, for twelve years, has operated an anti-social system of controls on school building, which condemn millions of our children to seek their education in out-of-date, insanitary buildings. Because schools simply have to be built in areas of new housing – or the children there would have no education at all – essential local authority programmes to replace the slum schools of our down-town areas fall under the Minister's axe. This is why we have insisted on the need for a steadily expanding industrial output and the operation of an appropriate system of priorities to ensure that Britain's rising industrial production is channelled into the areas of greatest social need.

That was what Swansea was about.

The picture I have painted tonight is drab and dingy, but millions of our people know it is not overdrawn.

That is why one of the most exciting tasks of the new Government will be a task of physical regeneration of our cities and towns and of some of the smaller industrial townships in the north and the midlands, dominated by slag heaps or other debris of Victorian industrialism.

It is not that there is no new building. The tragedy is that new building, which is geared to private profit and the speculative gains of the property developer, will, in the end, produce an asphalt and concrete wilderness.

It will be a shocking commentary on this age if, over the years, we get rid of the blighted areas we have inherited from the past and replace them with a newer and more expensive ugliness.

To achieve this rebuilding of Britain, three things are necessary.

The first – and I have dealt with this – is adequate machinery to get the land that is needed and on terms which ensure that land values created by the community accrue to the community.

The second is that the building industry should be mobilized for the immense task that lies ahead. Already this week, to judge from press reports, N.E.D.C. have expressed the gravest concern about the ability of the building industry to carry the load represented by the Government's own election targets.

This is one reason why we say categorically that in any pressure on building resources, area by area, less essential and speculative building must be held back to give the priority programmes the go-ahead.

But we shall need a much more dynamic approach to new building methods. After twelve years, the Conservatives are now intensifying work on prefabrication which some of us had carried a good way forward at the Ministry of Works in those early post-war years. Again, twelve years have been lost. But we shall need a great deal more planning of the supply of building materials – already bottlenecks are developing before the building programme really gets under way. And we shall need a much more progressive attitude to the problem of industrial training, including apprenticeships. Both sides will need to rid themselves of attitudes which derive from a generation of unemployment and casual work. Left to themselves, building employers, with some honourable exceptions, will not take on the numbers of apprentices required.

Apprenticeship will have to be more and more with the industry rather than with the individual firm.

Our proposed National Building Corporation – of which the Government's last-minute National Building Agency is a faint carbon copy – will be armed with real powers to get ahead with the job. To encourage new methods, there is a lot to be said for handing over the building programme of a complete new town to one or more big contractors who are prepared to use non-traditional methods; because such methods are priced out of the market if restricted to contracts based on penny-numbers. Factory methods involve a big layout and demand secure orders for years ahead.

The third need is a big breakthrough in Government organization. This may be unpopular with some local authorities, but it is becoming clear that the major decisions of land allocation and town and country planning will have to be taken by the Government. In area after area, we have seen delays of five years and more through the inability of local authorities to agree, particularly where major overspill programmes were involved. In the event, the matter has had to be resolved by the Minister, and it is not unusual at some of the major Ministry inquiries for twenty or thirty local authorities to be involved.

Provided that there is statutory provision for full consultation with local authorities, we can save years of delay and acrimony if the responsibility is placed directly on the Minister. He gets the ultimate odium anyway, so why should he not get it five years earlier? And once an area has been zoned, the Crown Lands Commission can get to work and acquire the land, thus saving years more.

So far as the major areas of the country are concerned, most of the facts are known: what we now want is action and decision.

But this job cannot be done from Whitehall. Regional regeneration and urban renewal will require a courageous degree of administrative decentralization. All the major Ministries concerned will have to have regional officers of high rank and standing to whom the maximum authority must be delegated, subject only to the ultimate control by the Minister and by Parliament.

In every region, we shall need to reconstitute the interdepartmental committees dealing with development. Where the problem is industrial development, the Board of Trade Regional Officer will be in the lead, though here we shall have very quickly to link regional expansion plans with Neddy and the proposed Ministry of Production. Where planning and land use are involved, this will be a matter for the regional housing and planning officers with the fullest consultation and harmonization of plans for transport – road and rail – and industry.

Heaven knows, we shall make mistakes. You will never rebuild Britain unless you are prepared to. But, at any rate, we shall avoid the sordid, dingy achievements of a century ago and the urban sprawl which unplanned development is in the process of creating.

And we shall not succeed in this giant task unless we can call into action all our people – architects and planners, local authority representatives and traffic engineers, sociologists and town planners – to build the cities of the future in which people live a satisfying life and realize to the full the talents and potentialities within them.

5   Plan for Full Employment

A speech made at the Philharmonic Hall, Liverpool, on Sunday, 8 March 1964

... I do not find it difficult to think of facts on which this Government stands condemned, but if there were no others I would regard as deserving of the utmost censure and condemnation a system of society which, year in year out, even at a time of what they regard as a dangerously feverish boom, cannot provide employment for its school-leavers. So when Sir Alec comes to Liverpool, as I have challenged him to do, let him tour the unemployed youth centres which the authorities have set up to provide for the school-leavers and other young men for whom the Government has failed to find a job. There are enough people in this hall who remember those bleak years when, for them, to be a teenager meant the progress from school to the dole queue, or the scramble of ten kids chasing one blind-alley job. Are we to say in a so-called civilized community that thirty years after we are still to confront boys and girls leaving school, going out into the world for the first time, here in Lancashire, and the north-east coast, in the Welsh valleys, in Scotland, with the embittering realization that they are not wanted, that all the provision for their education is to end like this.

And there's something else I'd like to show Sir Alec. The conditions in which some of our old people, the disabled, the sick have to live under his Government's inhuman bureaucratic rules, inadequate pensions and N.A.B. scales, prescription charges – our people are not having their fair share of Britain's slowly rising production, to enable them to live in their old age in the dignity to which their work in the past has entitled them. Two million on N.A.B. ... Local authorities, welfare organizations, and private individuals do a wonderful job, but their work is made the less effective because the Government compels them to work against a climate of poverty.

Another question for Sir Alec: In the post-election economic crisis of 1956, the then Chancellor Mr Macmillan introduced individual prescription charges. In the never-had-it-so-good atmosphere of the 1959 election, the Government refused to repeal these charges, as apparently the country would have gone bankrupt. In 1961, in the last crisis, these charges were doubled. Now, says Sir Alec, the economy has never been stronger. If he believes this, will he now announce his plans to celebrate by removing these unjust burdens from people who are least able to bear them? And if the economy is as strong as he says why then can we not afford invalid chairs and cars for paraplegic ex-miners and other disabled industrial workers here in Lancashire and the rest of the country? There are plenty of resources to provide expense accounts, and it all comes out of the same national pool, but this never-had-it-so-strong country will be bankrupt if we provide a few cars for men who have sacrificed their health and ability in working for their fellow men or if we provide the means of transport for what the Ministry of Health in their inhuman bureaucratic language call the below-knee amputees of two world wars.

There is another problem we should like to show him (he probably does not think it matters very much): the problem of bus passes for old-age pensioners. The old-age pensioners in my constituency in the main have not got chauffeurs and were provided by the Liverpool Corporation with free bus passes until 1954 when a Tory Council in Birmingham took the whole case to the High Court and got it declared illegal. So a Labour Member of Parliament, Ted Short, of Newcastle, introduced a Bill to make it legal, and it was half-way through the House of Commons when Sir Anthony Eden announced that we must have a General Election because we had just got a new Prime Minister. And we in the Shadow Cabinet pleaded with the Government to let that go through. In the end they let it through on one condition: that it should apply only to those routes that were in existence and on which free bus passes were valid in November 1954. Since then bus routes cover practically the whole of Kirkby, and they've built other housing estates around Liverpool, around Manchester, in all our big towns and cities, and only those pensioners living in houses on bus routes where there were free bus passes in November 1954 are entitled to get one. What does this mean? If this very afternoon there are constituents of mine and other Members on this platform who want to go off and visit their sons and daughters – perhaps they live in Kirkby and want to go to Speke – what is it going to cost them? It is beyond the reach of someone living on the miserably inadequate pensions that this Government awards them. But when Ted Short and Bessie Braddock and other colleagues here, and I, presented a Bill to the House of Commons to remedy this injustice Tory Members have killed it, Friday after Friday. When we have taken it to successive Ministers of Transport – Harold Watkinson, Ernest Marples – they have refused to give it Government backing. Now here is an example, it may be only a small one, you may not think it is important. Sir Alec certainly won't think it is important – he wouldn't understand what it is about – but the old-age pensioners of this area think it is important, an example of the fundamental inhumanity of the Tories in an age of unrivalled economic potential.

May I say on this: all right we can't get this through as backbench Members, as Opposition Members, but the next Labour Government is pledged as a Government measure to introduce this at the earliest opportunity.

But Sir Alec is too busy trying vainly to convince the voters that the Conservative Party has really changed its spots, that after twelve years in which we get after each election three years of stagnation and crisis, followed by a carefully engineered pre-election boom, they really do believe in expansion now, not just one year in four but all the time. They are relying on this election boom – which is already beginning to develop the usual import strains, even before the election – to induce people to forget 1961 and the pay pause, and the brutal interference with established wage bargaining and arbitration procedures, the nurses, the teachers, the railwaymen, the unemployed which their policies created. Because their secret weapon on which they count is short memories. And your job is to keep the facts before our people. This is why I want to use the rest of the time available to me this afternoon to deal with a problem of vital concern to this area, to the north-west generally, to the north-east, to Cumberland, to Scotland, to Wales, and to hard-hit parts of the south-west: the problem of employment and industrial and social regeneration.

Except in wartime we have not had full employment in these areas. We came nearest to it in the years of the Labour Government, when a national policy of full employment and industrial expansion, combined with a determined and purposive use of development area policy, brought us within reach of solving the problem. In 1951 Merseyside and Clydeside, Tyneside and the Welsh valleys, were nearer an age of assured full employment than they have been at any time since. Areas and townships which the defeatism of pre-war Toryism had written off, condemned to decline and depopulation, had been given new hope; a generation which had known little beyond the dole queue had been given a vision of a new future; towns and indeed regions which had been by-passed by the brittle and limited prosperity of inter-war capitalism were given a new industrial virility and purpose.

Then came Tory freedom, the drift to the south; profit replaced purpose; financial manoeuvrings replaced industrial growth as the mainspring of the national economy; and these areas began to wilt once again. We have had promises from them from time to time – the 1959 election was fought on Tory pledges to bring work to these areas. With each election we have had fitful attempts to do better. But the drift has continued – decline, depression, and in more than one area depopulation.

That is why we pledge ourselves to say that the General Election of this year will be the beginning of a new deal to replace the pussyfooting procedures of this Government, the sterility of their White Papers, by purpose and real planning.

Three things are needed: one, a national economic policy to maintain a national tide of high production and employment; two, effective machinery to channel that tide to the arid and parched areas of underemployment; and thirdly, positive measures, based on national and regional planning, to achieve the industrial and social regeneration of these areas.

First, the national policy. Ask any City analyst or financial expert how he diagnoses the present economic situation. He will say the boom is getting out of hand; he will stress growing labour shortage in the south and midlands, his metaphors will range from 'pressing on the ceiling' to 'overheating', and his remarks will end by the usual references to the accelerator and the brake. (That's what's wrong with their driving, all brake and accelerator – and this year the accelerator with the hand brake on – forgetting that the best modern cars these days have got a steering wheel as well.)

It is precisely because Tory freedom has created the two nations, an over-congested south-east and a starved north, that once again we are facing national measures to slow down the boom when whole areas have as yet barely begun to emerge from the depression. You can't solve the problem of full employment without a powerful head of steam, a powerful head of national expansion. When I scheduled Merseyside as a development area fifteen years ago, I said then that these areas were like grim rocks, covered by a high tide, but at times of low tide left bare and stark. But just as you need national full employment to provide the head of water, you need a proper distribution-of-industry policy to ensure that you don't have to slow down the boom because it is getting out of hand in the southern parts of the country.

In my speech at Swansea, which survived a ruthless critique by the five industrialists on TV, I set out the basis of a national policy of full. employment and industrial growth. And warned by twelve years of stop-go, I stressed that financial measures would not create the changes in industrial structure needed for expanded export industries and import-saving industries. A higher Bank Rate may meet an immediate strain on sterling. It does nothing to dynamize our industry and expand export: quite the reverse – it holds back much needed capital investment and industrial modernization.

So first we need an economic policy based not on finance but on industrial purpose, and that is what *Signposts* is about. That is what all our plans are about for the creation of these new industries based on science, and for a more purposive approach to the physical and structural problems of industry.

Second, we need a determined policy to bring new industries to these areas. In 1945–51, 30 per cent of all new factory building in Britain came to the development areas. I'll give you the figures under the Conservatives. In 1952, 21.6 per cent; 1953, 17.6 per cent; 1954, 18.1 per cent; 1955, 15.6 per cent; 1956, 19.3 per cent; 1957, 22.3 per cent; 1958, 18.6 per cent; 1959, 22.1 per cent; in not a single year did they get anywhere near the average for new factory building in development areas that a Labour Government had maintained. Then in 1960 we had the Local Employment Act setting up Development Districts, and if these covered smaller areas than Development areas, don't blame me; blame Sir Alec and his colleagues. But taking the financial year since then, the percentage has been, for the financial year 1960–1, 10.7 per cent; 1961–2, 13.3 per cent; 1962–3, 16.8 per cent; and of course, the first nine months of 1963–4, pre-election year, 27.8 per cent.

Sir Alec is always asking for our policies. Our development area policy was set out in the House by our Shadow President of the Board of Trade, Douglas Jay, and, in case Sir Alec missed it, I'm going to remind him of our nine-point programme.

Point 1: schedule all underemployed industrial areas as single comprehensive development areas, without any muddled distinctions between growth areas on the one hand and development districts on the other. Then use all the necessary powers within them wherever they are needed.

Point 2: as an emergency crash programme, because we are in an emergency in these areas, build far more adequate-sized advance factories, not just factories of 10,000 sq. ft, and put them in the areas where unemployment is worse.

Point 3: use the existing financial powers, not just to give grants for basic services in the development areas; but let the Board of Trade itself embark once again on a really adequate scheme for the clearance of derelict sites with a 100 per cent grant from the central Government. Let that go not merely for the north-east coast and Scotland, but to Wales, Merseyside, and west Cumberland as well.

Point 4: use the Industrial Development Certificates as effectively as they were used before 1951; and get the development areas' and Northern Ireland's share of the total factory building in the country back at least to where it was in the first years after the war.

Point 5: tackle the London office problem effectively, either by applying the I.D.C.s to offices, by decisively strengthening local authority powers, or if necessary by establishing building licensing in the congested regions only. And, incidentally, allocate all suitable London railway sites to housing.

Point 6: establish a real regional organization, with regional controllers of each of the Departments concerned in each regional capital, working regularly together and directly linked once more with the local authority town planning machinery.

Point 7: be prepared to steer to these development areas not just private projects but new projects launched either in partnership between private and public enterprise, or by public enterprise alone. The Government cannot say that this is impracticable.

Point 8: transfer more central Government offices to needy areas.

Point 9: organize now a really far-reaching programme for credits to developing Commonwealth countries, to be spent on surplus capacity in the United Kingdom.

Now that was Douglas Jay's nine-point programme, and that is the answer to Sir Alec's challenge to us on our policy, because if those nine points were put into effect we would very quickly have this problem of local employment under control.

Thirdly, industrial and social regeneration of areas such as Lancashire.

We are not going to solve our regional problem merely by diverting a few firms from the south to the north. The Tories rely on sporadic bribes to private industry to set up branches here. We want to see new industries, reflecting local needs and local inspiration. In my Scarborough speech I indicated how this could be achieved. I mentioned the chemical engineering industry, because I for one am getting tired of seeing new breakthroughs pioneered by British chemists and scientists, only to find the industrial development and the job of making the plant too often done by the engineering industries of America and Germany. Why shouldn't our engineers have a go? Last June in Moscow, when I discussed East-West trade with Mr Khrushchev and his colleagues, they told me then of orders of up to £100 millions – and indeed more – for chemical engineering. They don't want to buy the know-how, or pay us royalties. They want a complete turn-key job, ready to switch on. In Eastern Europe and the Commonwealth we are losing opportunities – this is why I have suggested a State-sponsored consortium, ensuring that we have the capacity to do the planning, design, and the engineering drawings so that the job of fabrication is done by British workmen and not by Germans and Americans on the basis of British invention. Think how our underemployed shipbuilding, marine engineering, and boilermaking capacity could be employed on sub-contracts for such a consortium. And think what a difference it would make to our exports.

Another example: why should not some of our redundant capacity in railway workshops or even Royal Ordnance Factories be turned to work for Commonwealth development? Or another idea: that new industries be based on science, which is such a central feature of Labour Policy in the 1960s. We want to link this with our new universities and colleges of advanced technology, and with the new ones we are going to build, as the spearhead of our new regional industrial drive. I have said recently that our new universities and other colleges should go not to our beautiful cathedral cities but to our industrial areas, gaining from them vigour and virility and a down-to-earth industrial inspiration.

We plan to place research and development contracts in the civil field with the technological departments of these universities and these colleges of advanced technology, and as they develop their research they can sub-contract to establish local industries, and then as research leads to a new breakthrough in industrial techniques – it won't in every case, but it will in some – this can lead to the creation of a new locally based industrial complex to exploit it, and help exports, import-saving, and local employment at one and the same time. That is one aspect.

The other aspect is social reconstruction. It is sometimes said that industrial Lancashire, in common with other areas, needs a face-lift. So it does, but it needs to go a lot more than skin-deep. Whether it is the removal of the slag heaps, the reclamation of new industrial land and housing sites from the ugly debris of nineteenth-century industrialism, or the reconstruction and redevelopment of city centres and some of the smaller industrial townships of these areas, this is going to need planning, and planning in the most dynamic and imaginative manner. It is not that nothing will be done if it is going to be left to Conservative freedom. But that will be done which earns a quick profit or capital gain, and it will be done – this is already happening – in a manner which will turn the Victorian ugliness that we have inherited into the profitable but aesthetically revolting asphalt and concrete wilderness with which, unplanned, we are threatened.

And we can't talk about regional development without bringing in transport, road and rail services between towns, and the replanning of our cities in the Buchanan age.

If ever I were in danger of attributing sincerity to the Conservative conversion to planning, Mr Marples and the Beeching programme would soon have disillusioned me.

I have made it clear that we do not criticize Dr Beeching. The fault lay not in the answer he gave, but in the question he was set. His report is a highly efficient and antiseptic job of surgery, because surgery is what the Minister told him to do. Modern medical practice suggests diagnosis should precede the remedy – whether that remedy is medical or surgical.

And because he was enjoined to look on the job as a narrow book-keeping, accountancy operation, this is what we got, with no regard for either social considerations or national or regional economic planning. Who would have thought that a Government that believes in planning, which has set up N.E.D.C., would have put through the Beeching report without consulting Neddy? without asking Neddy what would be the effect of 4 per cent expansion per annum – if they really mean to get it – on the revenue and the earning power of British Railways and of the transport system? Who would have thought that they would have failed to ask Neddy what effect these railway cuts will have on our programmes for industrial growth and similarly for regional development and development area policy?

Following the Report, we have had the hearings of the Transport Users Consultative Committees, and they are a complete farce, as we said they would be when during the debates on Mr Marples's 1962 Bill we sought to give teeth to the T.U.C.C.s. They have no power to examine the figures of 'losses' or operating costs, still less to balance the saving to British Railways of closure against the social costs in terms of providing additional roads, additional bus services or road haulage services, or the cost of congestion – and indeed the cost of human life which will result from these closures. Still less can they think in terms of regional development programmes. Mr Marples, in accepting this week the closure of two thirds of the lines on which these T.U.C.C. investigations have been held, has shown that he has little more conception of the national and regional issues involved than he allows the T.U.C.C. to have in their cramped terms of reference.

We have said what we shall do. We shall halt the main programme of rail closures – allowing, as we have said, individual closures to take place in one or two clear cases – pending a national transport survey, relating the railway programme to the needs of national and regional expansion, and to the requirements of a national integrated transport policy, covering roads and other forms of transport as well as railways.

Second, we shall create an integrated transport system, not a system of transport *apartheid*, in which profits on road and rail can be integrated, instead of allowing road haulage to cream off the more profitable traffics.

Third, we shall ensure a redistribution of traffic between road and rail, so that traffics will go on the means of transport which is most economic in national and social terms, instead of following the dictates of short-run private profit and bureaucratic railway book-keeping.

If we are to have all the benefits of regional planning, industrial and social, making the best use of our transport services, of our scarce resources of land, of local amenities, we are going to need revolutionary changes in the machinery of regional planning. What we feel will be needed I set out in a speech at Leeds a month ago. It will mean greater courage in national decisions, a very considerable degree of devolution of Whitehall's machinery to the regions, and statutory provision for effective consultation with those concerned, elected representatives and officials in local government.

In our biggest problem areas we shall need more than this, and considering the formidable job with which we shall be faced in industrial development, basic services, and social regeneration, we shall be forced to consider the establishment of authorities which reflect the imagination and comprehensiveness of President Roosevelt's Tennessee Valley Authority. Nothing less will be adequate.

For the task on which we are engaged is the most exciting one a people can take in hand on behalf not only of the Britain of today, but also of our children, of the Britain of tomorrow.

There will be here a challenge for every one of us. And the most exciting thing will be the prospect it holds out of releasing the energies and mobilizing the talent of the whole of the British people. It means a chance for the administrative skill and humanity of the best of our people in Local Government, in design and science, our skill in industry – above all it means through our educational system at all levels the development of the latent talent of millions of our children who in the past have never been given a place in the sun.

But there is one condition. It is that everyone of us works with confidence – but not complacency – with dedication, with the spirit that carried us through in 1945, to ensure that when this timorous, shrinking Government finally plucks up enough courage to put the issue to the test we do everything in our power to ensure that, after the twelve wasted years, drifting in the shallows, we are ready to take the Government of Britain into the hands of the people of Britain, and begin the task of creating the confident and assertive new Britain we shall be proud to hand on to those who will follow in our steps.

A speech at the Niblett Hall, in the Temple, on Monday,
20 April 1964, to the Society of Labour Lawyers

Tonight, I want to get away from the more highly publicized
political controversies of the day and dwell on a fundamental
difference of attitude between ourselves and the Conservatives.
The Labour Movement stands for the Rule of Law in both the
domestic and international spheres. We opposed the Tories over
Suez, not merely because we thought the whole enterprise was
misconceived but because it represented a resort to naked force
in defiance of the law of nations. When in the following year the
Conservative Government surreptitiously withdrew Britain's
signature to the optional clause of the International Court, we
denounced their action as soon as the fact became known.

If you look through the records of Parliament during the last
ten years, you will find that it is always the Labour Members
who have protested when African leaders in colonial territories
have been arrested without charge and detained without trial. It
was we who denounced Hola, and the creation of police-state
methods in Nyasaland. It was we who vigorously defended the
Devlin Report in the Commons Debate when that was under
attack by the then Attorney-General, the present Lord Chancellor, in a speech the level of which added little credit to him, his
office, or the Government.

We know, as Nye Bevan said, that politics is about power.
But we are against arbitrary power. In international no less
than in domestic affairs, our aim is to transfer power from the
litigants to the law. That is why we have consistently sought to
build up the authority of the United Nations.

This, indeed, has always been the attitude of the Labour
Movement. As long ago as 1929, a Labour Lord Chancellor,
speaking at the Mansion House, used these words:

Amid the cross currents and shifting sands of public life the law is like a great rock upon which a man may set his feet and be safe, while the inevitable inequalities of private life are not so dangerous in a country where every citizen knows that in the law courts, at any rate, he can get justice.

But if the law is to be, as Lord Sankey said, a great rock, and if public confidence in the law is to be maintained, then the law must keep abreast of the changing needs of our time. Nothing brings the law and the administration of justice into more disrepute than statutes and doctrines which are clearly out of date. That is why the next Labour Government will consider with all possible despatch the machinery of law reform.

For whatever our achievements in terms of economic or social policy, in housing, health, pensions, education, in foreign and Commonwealth affairs, in the machinery of our national Government, or the creation of a new system of regional planning, it is our determination that the next Labour Government will go down to history as one of the great liberal reforming administrations of this century, challenging comparison with any of the past.

Let me remind you in passing of what we did accomplish between 1945 and 1951. Since the passing of the Judicature Act in 1873, no government has accomplished more in this sphere. We replaced Workmen's Compensation by Industrial Insurance. In so doing, we got rid of the provision under which a man who accepted compensation was deemed to have 'elected' and so forfeited his right to sue for damages. Every lawyer and every trade-union organizer knew the many cases of injustice which were the result. Then we abolished the doctrine of common employment which had been an excrescence on the law for over a hundred years. You may remember the old saying 'Lord Abinger planted it, Baron Alderson watered it, and the Devil gave it increase.'

We passed the Crown Proceedings Act, a measure which had been in draft for twenty years but which successive Conservative Governments had refused to touch. For the first time, it became possible to sue a Government Department, in the same way as a private individual. Lastly, and perhaps most important of all, we were responsible for the establishment of legal aid. By so doing, we went further than any government had ever gone to remove the familiar reproach that 'The Courts are open to everyone – like the Ritz Hotel.'

Now, it would be absurd to pretend that law reform has been completely neglected since we left office or that useful measures have not been passed. I have in mind, in particular, the Tribunals and Enquiries Act which was welcomed from the Labour benches, although some of us felt that it did not go far enough. But law reform is extraordinarily uncertain and sporadic. It is not that we have lacked high-powered inquiries, marked by devoted and dedicated work, and leading to forward-looking reports of great authority. Some branch of the law comes into question. A committee of eminent jurists and others is appointed. They take evidence from those qualified to give it. They produce a unanimous or near unanimous report. Then the curtain falls. Unless a private Member who has been fortunate in the ballot is prepared to sponsor a Bill, the report lies in some unregarded pigeon-hole while the dust of years settles on it.

Let me remind you of one example. One of the anomalies of criminal law is the verdict 'Guilty but insane'. According to our notions of criminal responsibility, this is a contradiction in terms. It was only inserted in the Act of 1883 on the insistence of Queen Victoria. As long ago as 1923, the Atkin Committee recommended that this verdict should be abolished. We had similar recommendation in 1952 and again, this time from the Sellers Committee, last year. Now nobody, so far as I know, is prepared to resist the recommendations of the distinguished committee or to justify the law as it stands. Yet the verdict has remained for all these years.*

Let me remind you of one other example. In 1958, the Tucker Committee unanimously recommended that the evidence given at preliminary inquiries before the Magistrate should not be published in the Press until after the proceedings are completed either by the verdict at the trial or by the Magistrates refusing

*In the event, the month after this speech the Government introduced a measure abolishing this form of verdict.

to commit. This was a matter of very considerable importance. Last year a fuller inquiry was announced which, in a sense, may be said to have supplanted Tucker. It certainly reinforced Tucker. But until then the recommendations remained filed away in the Home Office, and the mischief which they were intended to cure remained and remains unabated.

Why is it that reforms of the law always have to take their chance? The familiar excuse is shortage of Parliamentary time. This I do not really believe. It is true that some measures, which may appear to lawyers to be matters of pure law reform, can arouse considerable interest and opposition among non-lawyers. A fairly recent example was a private member's Bill to extend compulsory road traffic insurance to include liability towards passengers. There are, however, many measures of reform which do not involve large questions of policy and need not, in fact, occupy the House of Commons for long.

We do not believe that the administration of justice should always be relegated to the end of the Parliamentary queue. The Society of Labour Lawyers have recently sponsored a book which I have read with deep interest – *Law Reform Now*. You will not expect me to comment on every one of its proposals. But there is one project which especially appeals to me. That is the creation of a body of Law Commissioners, replacing the Lord Chancellor's Law Reform Committee, to keep the whole field of possible law reform under continuous review. As a result of their advice there might indeed be an annual measure of law reform, just as in each Parliamentary session there is a Finance Bill and the Expiring Laws Continuance Bill.

Parliamentary time will have to be found for it. In my view, substantial measures of law reform – so much of which is un-controversial, and certainly unlikely to raise passionate feelings among lay Members of the House – could be got through with adequate consideration in the late evening, when the main business of the day is done.

There is, in my view, another opportunity, and we are pre-paring to take advantage of it. In the first few weeks of a new Parliament, when the Government's main measures are still being drafted – and really major measures can take up three months or even longer – there is a danger of a prolonged hiatus, a legislative vacuum with an urgent need for Bills to be introduced into both Houses, for a productive Parliamentary session means a number of Bills starting their progress in the Lords. A continuing Government is able in each session to prepare a number of Bills, major or minor, for introduction immediately after the Speech from the Throne. An incoming Government has no such advantage. Nor, I think, will there be much left in the Departmental pigeon holes on the departure of the present administration. They have pretty well scraped the barrel already, and the need to find additional work, when the Resale Prices and the Finance Bills are through, to keep the Mother of Parliaments from taking up knitting in Sir Alec's period of self-reprieve, will no doubt complete the process. We expect to find a scorched-earth situation, and we are, therefore, urgently considering new measures. This will provide a heaven-sent opportunity to the law reformers within our ranks, and here I pay tribute to the Society of Labour Lawyers for all they have done and are doing.

You will not expect me to give you an advance hand-out of the Queen's speeches for the next five years. Nevertheless, there are some matters with which a Labour Government would certainly deal. We are pledged to introduce legislation against racial incitement and discrimination. This would already have been dealt with if the Government had only given time to Fenner Brockway's Bill. We shall need to amend the Fugitive Offenders' Act – even the Home Secretary accepts the need for that – and deal with the general treatment of offenders coming from Commonwealth or foreign countries. We shall embark upon prison reform and remodel the system of punishment.

The Government, after twelve and a half years, have announced the appointment of a Royal Commission. This is to be welcomed, though we regard the terms of reference as a little myopic. But, as we made clear last week, we do not feel that the Government of the day should be held back from introducing long-overdue reforms by reason of the fact that the Royal Commission will be sitting. And we are fortunate in that the high-powered and industrious working party presided over by

Lord Longford, and including some now on this platform, together with many who possess a national reputation in matters of penal reform, crime prevention, and social affairs, has now nearly completed its work and will be reporting shortly.

This brings me to the Homicide Act. I think that it is generally agreed now that the Homicide Act has neither a rational nor a moral basis and few can be found to defend the present law. We feel that, as this is an issue on which people have strong views and which is to some a matter of conscience, it should be left to a free vote of the House, and we are prepared to find Government time for it. I think that on this sort of issue the House of Commons is at its best when each Member is expressing his own individual view.

We shall reform the law of landlord and tenant, especially in relation to the Rent Acts and to leasehold enfranchisement. We shall have to reconsider the Trades Disputes Acts following the recent decision of the House of Lords in Rookes *v.* Barnard. We shall consider criminal appeal procedure in the light of the recommendations of the Donovan Committee. We shall legislate for consumer protection.

Substantial changes will be needed in company law. It was the Jasper affair during the last General Election which led to the Government pledge to set up the Jenkins Committee, though most students of these matters have been disappointed with the outcome. The chapter on Company Law Reform in the book edited by Lord Gardiner to which I referred a few moments ago raises some very big issues, on which I do not wish to comment today. But on both mergers and take-overs, on monopoly powers, and the totally inadequate information directors are required to give to shareholders, legislation will be needed. Equally – though this, too, involves deep issues of policy as much as it involves modernization of the law – the next few years must see thoroughgoing measures to get rid of the moss and barnacles from our tax system.

So far I have been dealing in the main with bringing the law up to date. Of no less importance is the spirit in which we approach the task of administration and administrative machinery.

We have made it clear that we shall introduce new forms of planning. We shall plan for the use of all our national resources. But it has never been our intention that the ordinary citizen should be at the mercy of the planners. The more that the limitations of public responsibility are extended and recognized as necessary, the more essential does it become, as a counterpart, to make certain that the legal and other provisions which safeguard the rights and liberties of the individual are maintained and extended. In this respect both Parliament and the Courts have their part to play. But never must the individual feel that he is helpless against the great juggernaut of the modern state.

In this country we have two great traditional safeguards for the rights of individuals. There is the Parliamentary safeguard and the fact that Ministers can always be called to account in the House of Commons.

One of the reasons for our deep concern in recent years has been the casual attitude of certain Ministers to Parliamentary as well as to legal processes. We have a Home Secretary not notable for either his humanity or his liberality – Carmen Bryan, Soblen, Enaharo, the Williams family. In their way such episodes are as destructive of our democracy as any we have suffered. When the gods seek to destroy Governments they first tempt them into illiberality. For the misuse of power arising from the arrogance of office first manifests itself in straining, debasing, constitutional processes, not least in those cases where Ministers are entrusted with quasi-judicial functions.

The question has been raised in recent years whether the existing processes of parliamentary scrutiny are enough. For some time we have been examining suggestions for a parliamentary commissioner, on the lines of the Comptroller and Auditor-General, reporting to and through a Committee on the lines of the Public Accounts Committee. Some of us, with experience of that Committee, had thought of this as a possibility even before these ideas were publicly canvassed. There are difficulties, but I am hopeful we may have proposals to put forward.

In addition to the parliamentary safeguard there is the judicial safeguard.

We for our part are on the side of Coke and against Bacon. We entirely accept the contention that the function of the judges is to stand between the citizens and the Executive. It may be that we shall need to exercise greater control over the national economy. We shall ensure that the basic resources of the industrial capacity of this country are used not for the purposes of a few people but in the interests of the whole community. But we shall do it in the context of a free society in which Courts and the lawyers have their essential part to play.

In this context I must refer to the problem of crown privilege in respect of departmental documents. This whole subject needs a fresh look, for there is little doubt that departmental convenience too often overrides the needs of justice. Pending such an examination, and it must be thorough and will take time, I believe that as an administrative arrangement, by a directive from No. 10, it should be provided that no Minister should claim Crown privilege in such cases without reference to the Prime Minister – or perhaps it should be the Lord Chancellor. For too often one feels that the decision is made at departmental level, and that the Minister rubber-stamps it without having to justify the decision outside the Department.

Finally I come to the wider question of the United Nations and Human Rights. The extent to which human rights are being and have been trampled upon in different parts of the world – at the moment South Africa is the worst example, though unfortunately events in some other places in Africa give cause for grave concern – calls for urgent re-examination of the role of the United Nations in this field.

After the last war, when the details of the genocide and mass slaughter perpetrated by the Nazi racialists came to be known, the Attlee Government actively supported two historical actions to deal with this threat to civilized survival.

Firstly, the Charter of Nuremberg embodied the conception that international law was not only concerned with relations between states, that crimes against humanity were crimes against international law, and that human rights, that is to say, the basic rights of all men, everywhere, were rights international law should protect by, if necessary, punishing those responsible for infringing them.

Secondly, the Attlee Government – and in this endeavour it received notable support from another Labour Government, that of Australia – tried to create in the Commission on Human Rights appointed by the Economic and Social Council of the United Nations, in 1946, effective international machinery to deal with violations of human rights.

In this event, agreement was only reached on the Universal Declaration of Human Rights. Since those days, very little progress has been made at the United Nations with the attempt to agree a Convention on Human Rights and to establish machinery for its implementation and enforcement. I know how difficult it is to codify in forms that can be enforced the declarations of principles contained in the Declaration, though an example has been set by the European Convention. Nevertheless, I feel that in some fields, especially in race relations and the rights of women, more progress could be made. In my view, too, we ought to ratify the genocide convention which still awaits a British signature. This is a propitious moment for a British Government to take a fresh and vigorous initiative in the Human Rights Commission.

7　　Britain and World Peace

A speech at Bridgeport University, Connecticut, U.S.A., on Tuesday, 3 March 1964

The occasion of my last visit to the United States was to attend the funeral of the late President Kennedy. This nation which has recovered so remarkably from the shock of his sad and sudden death has no need to be reminded of his greatness. It is, in fact, two of his many remarkable speeches which inspire what I want to say today. It was on July 4th, 1962 – 186 years after your Declaration of Independence – that John Kennedy made his great challenge to the Western nations with his declaration of interdependence. As he said, the Declaration of Independence 'unleashed a revolution in world affairs'. The doctrine of national independence has swept through the world. But, he said, there must now be a new clarion call – for the interdependence of nations. America, he said, must begin to think intercontinentally. And he challenged Europe to do likewise.

It was a great challenge – and it's time we revived the concept. We must put aside our petty differences and nationalistic tendencies. We must create a partnership in the West which will not only cement our unity of purpose on so many great issues but will enable the Western nations to play a fuller part in the great tasks of world reconciliation.

The second speech which comes to mind today is one he delivered at the American University in Washington on June 10th, 1963. In a few simple words he awoke us from the long night of cold war propaganda and recrimination. He appealed directly to Mr Khrushchev to join in a new attempt to lift the burden of fear from the world.

I was in Moscow at the time, and two days after the President had delivered his speech I was discussing East–West relations with Mr Khrushchev. He was clearly deeply impressed by Kennedy's sincerity and understanding.

I believe this was a turning point. It was at that moment, ten days before the Chinese delegation were due to arrive to see if their differences could be patched up, that Khrushchev took what I think will be seen to have been a historic decision. He was at the parting of the ways. He could only repair his fences with the Chinese by a return to tough, cold-war talk with the West, perhaps even by aiding the fulfilment of Chinese nuclear ambitions. He decided to withdraw his objections to the test-ban treaty. My colleagues and I urged upon him the importance of the Senate declaration on a motion by the Senator from Connecticut in favour of a ban in the three environments, space, atmosphere, and underwater, thus getting over the deadlock on inspection of underground tests. The Senate declaration provided the means; President Kennedy's speech guaranteed the background of trust. Had it not been that, at that crucial moment, the occupant of the White House in Washington held out his hand, who knows what alternative Khrushchev would have accepted.

Those speeches are linked in my mind. Kennedy never saw the role of the Western Alliance in any narrow, restricted, inward-looking sense. The challenge was not to combine our resources for our own gain alone, but to enable us to make a fuller, more effective contribution to peace and prosperity in the world. And that is the theme I want to develop this afternoon in the short time at my disposal.

When Nato was formed, sixteen years ago, we were faced with a military threat of frightening proportions. Stalin ruled in the Soviet Union, and he sought to extend Russian influence deep into Western Europe. Had we not stood together then, Truman, Marshall, and Acheson here, Attlee and Bevin in Britain, the free world might not have survived. From the Nato military pact and the massive programme of Marshall Aid to Europe, which found its organizational expression in the Organization of European Economic Cooperation, has grown an alliance of nations concerned not only with their own defence and well-being but with the wider problems of a world struggling against the twin fears of war and hunger.

But the emphasis in these past years of cold war conflict has been on military preparedness. Vast resources in wealth and scientific knowledge have built up our nuclear power to such an extent that, between us, the destructive power of nuclear weapons amounts to about 50,000 megatons or the equivalent of fifteen tons of TNT for every man, woman, and child in the world. We could destroy the world many times over. The West could, and so could the Soviet Union. It was the clear realization that this was true that created the drama in the Cuban crisis in October 1962. It seemed that the two greatest powers in the world were on a collision course – but statesmanship prevailed and the world breathed again.

The danger that we face today is the proliferation of nuclear weapons. It is a danger with which we in the Labour Party have been concerned for several years. With technical advancement, nuclear capability is within the reach of many nations. France and China are in the race. Each new nuclear power may convince another that it cannot afford to be without them. If China, then India. If India, then Pakistan. If Egypt, then Israel. And if Britain and France assert the right to independent nuclear power in Europe then it will not be long before a similar claim is put forward by the Germans. In a world of two nuclear powers there are dangers, but the deterrent effect is strong. There is some measure of stability. In a world of many nuclear powers, with new nations struggling for nuclear authority, the possibility that one of them would use it for the fulfilment of a nationalistic aim would create a situation of the acutest danger.

All of us would, of course, like to get rid of nuclear weapons altogether. We do not despair of this, but it is not an immediate possibility. It can only come as result of general and complete disarmament with international inspection. The next best thing is to make an attempt to restrict the nuclear club to two. With this in mind, Hugh Gaitskell argued the case for a non-nuclear club covering all nations except the U.S.A. and Russia. Obviously control is easier with two than with many. This is clearly the view of both the U.S.A. and the Soviet Union. As I have said,

I was frequently reminded when in Moscow last year that the U.S.S.R. could easily have patched up her quarrel with China if she had agreed freely to share nuclear information. And America could have done the same with France. Your Government sees the dangers, as we do.

This is a problem within the alliance and for the alliance in its dealings with the rest of the world. Within the alliance the pursuit of nationalistic nuclear aims will be divisive and encourage the centrifugal forces within Nato. In our relations with the outside world the proliferation of nuclear weapons in Europe makes East–West understanding infinitely more difficult. Above all, any move to confer nuclear power on Germany, directly or indirectly, would be likely to take us past the point of no return in dealings with a Russia which through history has had an obsessional hate-admiration feeling about the Germans.

This brings me to the proposed mixed-manned force. I fully understand the motives which prompted this proposal and I have said repeatedly in the House of Commons, in Washington, and in Moscow that if I were convinced that this is the only way to stop Germany becoming a nuclear power I would reluctantly go along with the proposal. But I am not convinced. We do not think it adds one iota to the deterrent striking power of the West. Whatever we in the West may lack we have no need for new nuclear weapons and delivery systems. The proposed force would be vulnerable to enemy attack. Ultimately, the decision to use nuclear weapons would be an American one. It would give the appearance but not the reality of shared nuclear control.

I fear that some of the participants would not for long be satisfied. So far from sublimating nuclear appetites it might whet them. Some would seek some means of majority control; other powerful voices in Europe have urged the need to create a European deterrent and see the M.L.F. as a step in this direction. In fact, some of those most vociferous in their arguments for European unity are today arguing the case for a European nuclear deterrent to put them 'in a position of equality' with the United States. This would split the alliance down the middle – but this has always been one of the dangers of European integration which was not fully understood in the United States. You have always hoped for a united Europe which would be a partner with the United States. Equally it might be a competitor. It has always been our view that the base of European unity was too narrow – too narrow in that it stopped short at neutral nations like Sweden and Austria – too narrow in that it stopped short at the Atlantic.

European unity, whether political or economic, which is a stepping stone to an Atlantic – indeed a free world – partnership, is one thing. A form of integration which encourages a narrow 'Little Europe' nationalism, an inward-looking mentality, whether in economic or in political terms, would be a danger to our alliance. The essence of the alliance is not separation but interdependence. Each nation within the alliance should make its most effective contribution as part of a team. We believe that Britain has a distinctive and unique contribution to make as a result of our historic role as a world power. The nature of our overseas commitments, resulting partly from our Commonwealth connexions, requires us to maintain a modern, highly trained, well equipped, and mobile army which can be available for service in situations such as exist in Cyprus, Malaysia, and East Africa. I believe the whole world has been impressed by the speed with which our troops were moved into critical situations in the past few weeks, and by their restraint and bearing in positions of great danger. In none of these situations would nuclear weapons have any relevance. No one would think of killing a mosquito with a hand grenade. At present our conventional capability is inadequate. And mobility means speed. I believe that in the remaining years of this century our historic role as a naval power is going to find a new fulfilment both in helping newly established nations and in moving rapidly and effectively in fulfilling an international police role. This means naval forces, and these cannot be afforded if we are spending our substance on the pursuit of illusory nuclear status.

We want, therefore, to concentrate our resources on our conventional contribution. And while we feel that our contributions will be more and more in Africa and Asia we must also effectively fulfil our commitments in Europe itself.

But the problem of European defence is not just a British or European problem – it is an American problem too. I think we have to find a means of a much closer sharing in policy-making concerning nuclear weapons within the alliance as a whole. This must imply a willingness by the United States to repose in her allies a greater degree of trust. That is what interdependence is about. This is a time when great concepts have to be put into concrete terms.

I should like to say a word about the new Germany. The achievement of democracy in modern Germany is one of the historic developments of the post-war world. The end of the Adenauer régime gives hope, limited so far, but hope, of a move from the rigid inflexible position of the past few years to more positive initiatives. New men, new philosophies in Germany deserve our support and our encouragement. In the past years the developing relations between the Labour Party on the one hand and Willy Brandt and his Social Democratic colleagues on the other have reached a point where we can say that the two greatest democratic socialist parties in Europe are closer than ever before. Looking at the next decade in Europe this development may prove to be as historic in the creation of international understanding and cooperation as the Common Market is in the supranational approach. We have also played a constructive part in aiding the establishment of the new coalition Government in Italy.

If to begin with I have stressed the importance of the health of our Western alliance, it is not because I am concerned only with the maintenance of our defences, vital though this is, but because I hold deeply that in the new era into which we are moving the challenge for the West is in fact the welfare not of one part of mankind but of the whole of mankind. We will fail in our task if we allow ourselves to become introspective, inward-looking, or narrow in our outlook. We are not, never have been, and never must allow ourselves to become a partnership of nations who wish to dominate. It is not our purpose to impose our will or even our political concepts upon the rest of the world. Our task is to liberate.

In the years that immediately followed the war, it may have

seemed to many that the first task was to liberate peoples from
the shackles of colonialism. So it was. When the United Nations
was formed, nearly half the world lived under foreign domination
– sometimes ruthless, sometimes benign, but still foreign domination. Great strides have been made in the granting of freedom to
former colonial nations. The very fact that sixty-two free and
independent states have come into the United Nations since its
founders signed the charter is proof of this achievement. In this
field, Britain has played an outstanding role: from 1947, when
India, Pakistan, and Burma gained their independence, to recent
months when Uganda, Tanganyika, and Kenya have come into
the family of nations.

When the history of this age of ours comes to be written
centuries from now I believe that the decision of Clement Attlee
and his Government to grant India its independence will be one
of the turning points in world history.

We may regret that these new countries have not all followed
us in our democratic way of life; whatever our anxieties we
must be patient and remember that in Britain's 700 years'
advance towards political democracy we went through many
autocratic aberrations, many lurches into the kind of interference
with freedom which we now rightly condemn in some of the
new nations. We cannot, however, show such tolerance in situations such as South Africa whose leaders have deliberately
chosen the course of racial oppression. We warmly welcome
your Government's decision, and that of the United Nations,
to cut off arms from South Africa.

The second task in our liberatory mission is to help the underdeveloped countries of the world to stand on their own feet.
We must do so without strings. We cannot buy their respect or
their political loyalty. We would think the worst of them if their
souls were for sale. We must help because it is right to do so.
The problems of the developing countries are immense – the
rapidly rising population, an acute shortage of skills and capital,
deep-rooted lack of integration between the various sectors of
their economy, unemployment and underemployment and inability to exploit their resources and to find overseas markets
for their goods, over-reliance on one or more products – prob-

lems too many to enumerate but which add up to a circle of misery, illness, and hopelessness. Yet in spite of greatly increased amounts of aid to the developing countries – the United States alone since the war has contributed $105 billion in aid – the gap between rich and poor grows wider. But we have two achievements to our credit in the preparation for what in the rest of this U.N. development decade must be a massive war on want.

First, the principle of the welfare state, which we socialists have pioneered, 'from each according to his capacity, to each according to his need', is beginning to be accepted in international affairs. More and more of the developing countries are accepting as an obligation that part of their wealth must go to help others.

Secondly, there is the beginning of the acceptance that the battle against poverty cannot be fought without international planning. Massive aid, generously given, can be wasted if it is not constructively utilized. We have to secure the willing and active cooperation of the peoples in the developing countries. This is not a relief programme. We are not talking about the begging bowl. We are talking about aid which will stimulate the economy, which will enable peoples to exploit their raw materials and their human resources, to improve their agriculture and to develop their industries. Private enterprise is not a sufficiently broad basis on which to start a self-generating process of expansion. In as much as foreign investors have exerted pressure against state enterprises, they may in the long term have harmed rather than helped the poor countries.

If it is argued that the price we pay for planning is high in terms of form-filling and controls, the price we pay for economic 'do as you please' is still greater as it culminates in unemployment and stagnation and sometimes revolution and disaster, as in the case of Cuba.

There is one thing we must understand. If we are scared away from demanding economic planning, then others will step in with their more rigid and dictatorial versions. The struggle for the soul of Asia is a struggle between the democratic socialism of India and the totalitarian Communism of China. That is why the

Labour Party took the lead in Britain in proposing a massive lend-lease programme to help India to resist Chinese aggression without imposing upon India the need to sacrifice urgent economic and social progress. This is why, too, we have committed ourselves to full support for Malaysia. For if India and Malaysia go under, or fail to make the breakthrough they seek in democratic economic development, then Asia goes under with them, beyond the hope of any Western intervention.

An essential part of our planning must be the removal of many of the present obstacles and barriers to world trade. For the developing countries, trade is far more important than aid. That is why we have pledged support to Mr George Ball's proposal for internationally agreed import quotas for Asian textiles and other manufactured goods. Thus, it is vital not only in the interest of industrialized countries but of the poor half of the world that we achieve some measure of success in the Kennedy Round of tariff negotiations and in the conference which starts later this month in Geneva on world trade and economic development.

If then our second task is to play our full part in freeing peoples of the world from the shackles of poverty, then our third must be to liberate mankind from the fear of war. There have been important steps forward since the test-ban treaty to which I have made reference. The 'hot line' between the White House and the Kremlin is one. Another welcome advance is the agreement of the two giant powers to ban the use of outer space for military purposes. Other proposals are now being debated at the disarmament conference in Geneva.

My Party has warmly welcomed the bold initiative of your President in the five proposals which he made in his message to the Geneva conference last month. Most important of all was his plan to halt now further increases in strategic armaments. He said that: 'The United States, the Soviet Union, and their respective allies should agree to explore a verified freeze of the number and characteristics of strategic nuclear, offensive and defensive vehicles.' We assume that this includes not only intercontinental ballistic missiles but intermediate range ballistic missiles too. To this has now been added the possibility of the destruction of obsolescent bomber aircraft. Both these proposals are ones that may receive the support of the Soviet Union.

There is another proposal to which we attach considerable significance – the suggestion that there should be a freeze on nuclear weapons in Central Europe – an agreement neither to manufacture nor to introduce additional stocks of nuclear weapons in East and West Germany, Poland, and Czechoslovakia. We welcome this as a step towards an area free of nuclear weapons and with controlled conventional forces.

To achieve further progress, I recognize, a heavy responsibility rests upon the Soviet Union to assist in providing facilities for effective inspection.

If we can achieve some more measures of disarmament we can free not only some of the industrial resources which go into the arms race but the technical and scientific skills, so that we may throw ourselves more vigorously and wholeheartedly into the struggle against poverty. Our aim must be the sublimation of the arms race into a no less challenging but friendly development race where East and West can vie with each other on the basis of their contrasting forms of society, to see which can do most to drive poverty and hunger from the world.

In these three great aims – liberation, peace, and prosperity – the Atlantic partnership must play its full part with other nations in the United Nations. In the Labour Party we believe that our ultimate aim is nothing less than world government. And the first step on this exciting route is the United Nations. It must be strengthened so that it can become a more effective guarantee of peace. Among other ways of increasing its peace-keeping capability we must now take steps to provide the United Nations with the nucleus of a permanent international police force. This will require the recruitment to the U.N. Secretariat of a headquarters staff and the earmarking by member states of specially selected and trained troops available on call for U.N. duty.

The pity is that the enemies of the growth of the United Nations are to be found as much in the West as in the Communist world. Some of them look back nostalgically to the days of colonialism and cannot face the world as it is today. Some of them, including the Soviet Union and France, are behind with their payments. What they – and Spain and Portugal can't be ignored in this context – lack in enthusiasm we must make up. We will play our parts: so will our friends in the Commonwealth.

This is the supreme link for the Atlantic community. When history is written we shall be judged by our contribution, not to our own wealth but to the general welfare of nations. The United Nations may stand as our memorial. If it be otherwise we may all perish.

A speech made in the House of Commons, moving an Amendment to a motion by the Prime Minister, 6 February 1964

Mr Harold Wilson (Huyton): I beg to move, to leave out from 'House' to the end of the Question and to add instead thereof:

regrets the continuing failure of Her Majesty's Government to take any constructive steps for the expansion of Commonwealth trade; deplores the damage done to economic relations with the Commonwealth by recent Government policies; and calls on Her Majesty's Ministers to prepare, as a matter of urgency, an effective plan for the development of Commonwealth production and trade.

Having listened to the Prime Minister's speech no words of mine could be more eloquent in support of our Amendment than the ones to which we have just listened. I am bound to say that we are ourselves to some extent at fault here, because when we put into our Amendment words about asking the Government '... to prepare, as a matter of urgency ...' we did not realize sufficiently, perhaps, until we heard the right hon. Gentleman, that the Government have no sense of urgency at all in this matter.

For an inspiring and challenging subject such as this is – and we have had some very challenging and inspiring debates about this in past years – the right hon. Gentleman's speech was completely flat and dispirited. So far as I could tell, he said only three things: first, that there had been some Privy Councillorships for judges in Australia and New Zealand; and we welcome it; secondly, that there were to be improved relations between our chambers of commerce and the Commonwealth chambers of commerce; and thirdly, that there would be increased provision for technical aid and the exchange of young people, teachers and others, with the Commonwealth. On that we very much welcome the announcement that has been made of the highly distinguished patronage that this scheme is to have. Most of us read about it in the press this morning, but that does not in any way diminish our pleasure that His Royal Highness is to head the scheme. Had we been consulted about this – and it was quite incorrectly stated in the press that we had – the only point we would have made is that, if His Royal Highness is to preside over it, it would have been fitting that we should have had a much more imaginative and dynamic scheme and not the tuppenny ha'penny one which the right hon. Gentleman has just announced.

The right hon. Gentleman showed by his speech – and here he has been to some extent consistent – that he had not much hope of increasing Commonwealth trade; he gave up the ghost years ago. Before I deal with some of the facts of the Commonwealth trade situation which he failed to present to the House, I would remind him of some words that he uttered in another place two and a half years ago, on 21 June 1961, in a debate on the Commonwealth and the Common Market. It will be remembered by the House that at that time the then Prime Minister kept telling us that the Cabinet had not taken any decision about entering into the Common Market.

That was not taken until 31 July, but the then Foreign Secretary had made up his own mind. He was out on his own. I should like to quote a few words to show the faint praise in the past with which he has examined the possibilities of Commonwealth trade:

Therefore, my Lords, on this economic side of the problem –

it will be understood that I am quoting –

which we are discussing, if we are to maintain our standard of living and consumption – and, of course, the ability of the United Kingdom citizen to consume has a direct impact on Commonwealth trade – and if we are to be in a position to export the capital for which the Commonwealth is hungry today, then we must ask ourselves – and the Commonwealth, too, must join in asking this question most seriously – whether we can afford to be excluded from this European market which is expanding so rapidly and offering so many opportunities.

The right hon. Gentleman then went on to discuss the change

which has taken place in the nature of Commonwealth trade, a point which he made again this afternoon. He said:

... a study of the trends and prospects leads me to the conclusion that we should be very unwise to turn our backs on the European Market, which is showing so much vitality. Because even if we succeed in expanding Commonwealth trade, we shall want the additional earnings that we could earn in European markets if we are to fulfil our duty to the Commonwealth. ... Therefore, I would conclude that while we should maximize our Commonwealth trade in every way we can – and I would commend to my Commonwealth colleagues and partners that they should study again the results of the Montreal Conference – at the same time, we should increase our earnings in Europe. It would be difficult to do that unless we were inside the Community.*

The right hon. Gentleman's argument at that time – and I believe that it is still at the back of his mind – is that we were not going to get very much out of increased Commonwealth trade and that, for the reasons that he gave and the careful analysis that he gave in another place, we had better hopes in the Common Market, and if we were there we should be able to do more for the Commonwealth.

The Prime Minister: The right hon. Gentleman has quoted extensively from a speech which seems to be very consistent with what I have said today. I would just mention that I do not see what he is getting at. I said that we wanted to maximize Commonwealth trade as far as we possibly could.

Mr Wilson: I said that I thought that the speech which the right hon. Gentleman made then was consistent with the speech which he made today. That was the whole point that I was trying to make. At that time, he was extremely defeatist about Commonwealth trade, and he was very defeatist about it today. At that time, his argument was that we could not do very much unless we were in the Common Market, and of course I must inform the right hon. Gentleman that we did not get into the Common Market. Despite the fact of the Government's capitulation on issue after issue affecting our ability to maintain imports from the Commonwealth – despite that – we did not get in.

*Official Report, *House of Lords*, 21 June 1961; Vol. 232, c. 624 and 626.

I propose to return to the Common Market issue, because I hope that the right hon. Gentleman will not continue to evade certain questions which I have put to him recently on this subject.

First, let us talk about the record. Our position on Commonwealth trade is on the record. It is on the record in Government and it is on the record in Opposition. Hon. Members opposite sometimes said during the Common Market debate that the Labour Party's support of Commonwealth trade was of recent origin. I refute that. I refute it by reference to our own record in Government, from 1945 to 1951, when Commonwealth trade as a proportion of our total trade was at an all-time record; and this did not happen by accident. It happened through purposively planned long-term contracts with Commonwealth countries. I refute it again by our refusal to sacrifice Commonwealth preferences. I myself, in April 1951 at the Torquay Tariff Conference, broke up that Conference at three o'clock in the morning on one issue: our refusal to give way to the American demand to dismantle Commonwealth preferences.

At the same time I stated on behalf of His Majesty's then Government that if G.A.T.T., which was then an interim agreement and due to disappear, was to become permanent, we should insist on removing the clause about new or extended preferences. It was also the Labour Government, through the mouth of Sir Stafford Cripps and Ernest Bevin and others, that publicly announced our willingness to enter a free trade area for the Commonwealth, and equally support of Commonwealth trade has been our consistent policy in over twelve years of opposition. It was we who opposed the Government's surrender to the clamorous demands they were facing for the restoration of speculative commodity markets when they scrapped the long term contracts which had done so much for Commonwealth trade.

It was we who over this period – not over the last few months – called for international commodity agreements which we as a Government had made a central feature of the Havana Charter.*

*Agreement to establish a world free trading system negotiated in 1947. With the failure of the U.S. Congress to ratify the Charter, the temporary, interim General Agreement on Tariffs and Trade (G.A.T.T.) was put into force, which despite its provisional nature has become a permanent body.

And when the Government consistently rejected the idea of international commodity agreements – and they were rejected with monotonous regularity – and they were still voting against commodity agreements at Geneva as recently as January 1962 – when this was happening, I would refer hon. Members to the attacks that we were making on them. I do not want to go too far back over past speeches, but I would refer the right hon. Gentleman, because I know he is interested in this subject, to look at the debate as long ago as 3 February 1953, eleven years ago. It was on that occasion that we put forward from this Box a comprehensive plan for Commonwealth trade, Commonwealth development, and commodity agreements; a plan that was turned down by the Government because they were more interested in commodity speculation.

Again, I refer to our defence of the Commonwealth interest throughout the Common Market negotiations when right hon. Gentlemen opposite – and we have made this statement before – were, quite honestly, breaking pledges which had been solemnly given to this House and to the electorate about Commonwealth trade.

Mr Nicholas Ridley (Cirencester and Tewkesbury): May I ask the right hon. Gentleman whether he would always put Commonwealth preference before joining the Common Market at any stage in the future? Does he realize that that would mean that a Labour Government could never join Europe if there ever were to be one?

Mr Wilson: I shall deal with the Common Market position at the end, and perhaps when I have dealt with it I might put the same question to the right hon. Gentleman and see what his answer is. I shall deal with the question of preferences.

Despite that diversion, I shall not be distracted from reminding the House that in successive debates on the Common Market – the right hon. Gentleman was not here but he can read *Hansard* on 7–8 November 1962, I quoted in full the particular pledges given by the then Prime Minister, the present Chancellor of the Exchequer, and the present Minister of Defence, over all the years that there would be no interference with Commonwealth trade. Those pledges are very much on the record. I do not want to weary the House by repeating them today, but if anyone denies that they were made I have them here ready to read them again.

The right hon. Gentleman referred to the Kennedy Round and its vital importance for the Commonwealth. I agree very sincerely indeed with the right hon. Gentleman, and during all the Common Market negotiations we kept on saying that this was the thing the Government should be aware of. We said that the Lord Privy Seal's hand would be much strengthened if they did not feel in Europe that we had to get in at all costs. We said that instead of the picture that was being built up of a Common Market including Britain on one side of the table and the United States on the other, why should not we look forward, if the Common Market negotiations became intolerable, as they did, to a situation where we had Britain, the United States, the Commonwealth and E.F.T.A. on one side of the table and the Six on the other? But right hon. Gentlemen were in such a rush to get into the Common Market at all costs that they rejected that. This is all on the record, and I do not want to weary the House by quoting debates and what we said and the Government's rejection of what we said, but in the debate of 11 February last year, after the Brussels breakdown, we stated clearly our line about the Commonwealth and about the Kennedy Round. Therefore, from 1945, nearly twenty years ago, we at least can claim a consistent record in this matter.

I still have not quite understood the right hon. Gentleman's motive in this afternoon's performance – whether it was to try to restore his party's tattered Commonwealth image or to get up and announce a conversion. There was not much sign of conversion. We do not need to come to the Box and announce a conversion. Our consistency over nineteen years in Government and opposition is a sufficient test of our sincerity.

But let us now look at the figures. If hon. Gentlemen opposite want to snigger about Commonwealth trade, let them snigger at the figures. The Government's Motion begins with the words 'Commonwealth trade'. We thought that we might hear something about it from the right hon. Gentleman, but we heard so very little. I thought that he might have looked at the figures and given them to the House. I shall do so instead. Pre-war our imports from the Commonwealth were 34 per cent of our total trade. Under a Labour Government, as a result of deliberate planning, they rose to 43 per cent. By 1962 they had fallen to 35 per cent. That was under the right hon. Gentlemen opposite. If we consider exports to the Commonwealth, we see that before the war 35 per cent of our total exports were to the Commonwealth. Under a Labour Government, 44 per cent of our exports were to the Commonwealth. In 1962 they had fallen to 32 per cent.

Of course, the Government have always excused themselves with the argument that from the trade point of view the Commonwealth is a declining asset, that there is an inevitable, inexorable, secular, downward trend. That was the theme of the Prime Minister's speech to which I referred. It was certainly the argument of the Chancellor of the Exchequer in the debate of August 1961 on the Government's decision to seek entry into the E.E.C. The decline in Commonwealth trade the then President of the Board, now Chancellor of the Exchequer, said was due to what he called historical reasons.

What were those historical reasons? One, of course, was the then President of the Board of Trade* and his predecessors. Another was the then Secretary of State for Commonwealth Relations† and his predecessors, and of course, as the Prime Minister reminded us, he himself was Secretary of State for Commonwealth Relations for about five years, I think it was from 1955 to 1960, and he might like to know – perhaps he did know at the time and has forgotten – that during that period imports from the Commonwealth as a percentage of total imports fell from 43 per cent to 36 per cent. That happened in the five years when he was charged with the stewardship of Commonwealth relations. He might like to know that over that period the total imports of this country rose by £680 millions, while imports from the Commonwealth actually fell by £22 millions – a pretty proud record!

This doctrine of the inevitability of Commonwealth decline has become part of the tribal mythology of the party opposite.

*Mr Reginald Maudling.   †Mr Duncan Sandys.

The argument – though I do not think that it would deceive anybody who studies the figures – is that the Commonwealth – whether the developing countries or the advanced countries – is making such progress in manufactures that we cannot hope to sell manufactured goods – even developmental capital – there any more, and so we must concentrate on Europe and the United States, whose manufacturing industries are far more developed than those of the Commonwealth.

If it is true that the growth of indigenous industries in the Commonwealth makes it impossible to increase our trade there, why is it that other industrial countries, the United States, Germany, Japan, and Sweden, have had such spectacular successes in Commonwealth markets in the past twelve years? Does the fault lie with the Commonwealth, or with ourselves? Why has our trade with the Commonwealth shown this comparative decline? What are these historical factors?

I think that there are two. First, the Government's action, or failure to take action, both in overseas trade policy – that was never mentioned this afternoon – and in their external economic policy; secondly, and with a few honourable exceptions, the mediocre record of wide sectors of British industry in the matter of seizing opportunities that are there and which more enterprising and vigorous manufacturers from other countries have seized, despite the preferential advantages that we enjoy, even today.

I dislike wearying the House with figures, but I felt that in preparing his speech the right hon. Gentleman had not given a great deal of study to the relevant statistics. One did not see evidence that he had spent many hours on it, so I hope that the House will bear with me while I go through the figures with him. From 1953 to 1962 total Commonwealth imports – that is all Commonwealth countries excluding the United Kingdom, Ireland, and South Africa; the last-named I have excluded throughout – from all countries over the past nine years has risen from £7,608 millions to £11,102 millions, an increase of 46 per cent. That is, the total of imports coming into all Commonwealth countries, other than Britain, has risen by 46 per cent, so there has been a rapidly rising market. But their imports from the

United Kingdom rose only from £1,076 millions to £1,208 millions – an increase of only 12 per cent, despite preferences.

Put in another way – while the imports of our Commonwealth partners have risen in total, over those nine years, by nearly £3,500 millions, their imports from us have risen only by £132 millions. We have, in fact, achieved one fortieth of this large increase.

Let us take the figures for each country. Only in Hong Kong have we maintained our share of the export market. In Canada, where some effort has been made as part of the dollar drive, imports from all sources rose by 36 per cent, and from Britain by 20 per cent; Australia's imports from all sources rose by 75 per cent and from us by 8 per cent; Ghana's imports from all sources rose by 62 per cent, and from us they dropped by 1 per cent; India's imports from all sources rose by 85 per cent and from us by only 2 per cent; Malaya and Singapore's imports from all sources rose by 43 per cent and from us by 12 per cent; New Zealand's imports from all sources rose by 42 per cent, and from us by 8 per cent; Nigeria's imports from all sources rose by 87 per cent, and from us by 17 per cent; and Pakistan's imports from all sources rose by 101 per cent and from us by 31 per cent.

Hon. Members may say that perhaps they were importing raw materials. In that case, let us take manufactured goods alone. Here I will take two separate periods – 1954–60 and 1961–2. In the period from 1954 to 1960 Commonwealth imports of manufactured goods from all sources of production rose by 50 per cent – by half – and from us by only 13 per cent. In 1961–2 – the last year for which figures are available – Commonwealth imports from all countries rose by 5·4 per cent, whereas from Britain they were down by 5·1 per cent.

If we take all the main groups of exports – chemicals, textiles, metals and miscellaneous metal manufactures, non-electric machinery, electric machinery, transport equipment, and 'other manufactures' – in every group, taking the period 1954–60 or the period 1961–2, our increase is less than that of all the other countries and, in most cases, very much less. Some of these are in sectors of industry where not long ago we led the world. I have the figures. They were published by the right hon. Gentleman's Department in a very interesting survey last September.

Taking all the separate figures for particular types of engineering equipment, we find an appalling comparison between our own export record and those of most other exporters to the Commonwealth.

Mr J. Harvey: The right hon. Gentleman has said that he does not want to worry the House with figures. He should guard against misleading the House with figures. Will he address himself to this question: he suggested that in India 80 per cent of the increase in trade has gone to other countries. Will he also tell the House how much of the fixed investment in India, made in years gone by, is British investment? Does it not follow that we cannot go on contributing at the same rate?

Mr Wilson: That was a very helpful intervention, showing exactly what is wrong with the party opposite. They spend their time living in the past and thinking that in these economic matters the world owes us a living because of what we did in the nineteenth century. I can give the House a lot of figures. But I give the hon. Member this point – which he did not make – in respect of the Indian figures. I agree that those figures were affected by the substantial tied American aid which caused an increase in American exports. But that is not true of most of the other countries or the other figures that I have given. The fault lies not in a failure of Commonwealth markets to expand but in our own failure to hold our share of those markets. We have been losing ground to our competitors.

I want to give one final set of figures. They are dollar trade figures. I take two of our principal competitors – the United States and Japan. In 1954, between them they supplied 1,010 million dollars worth of manufactured goods to the overseas sterling area, while we supplied 2,907 million dollars worth. That means that in manufactured goods supplied by the three leading countries in this regard – Britain, United States, and Japan – we accounted for nearly three quarters of the total trade. That was as recently as 1954, before the right hon. Gentleman became Secretary of State. In 1962 the figure for the United States and

Japan together had risen from 1,010 million dollars to 2,511 million dollars, while ours had risen only from 2,907 million dollars to 2,981 million dollars. Theirs increased by 1,500 million dollars, or 150 per cent, and ours by 74 million dollars, or $2\frac{1}{2}$ per cent. If we put it in another way, we had three quarters of the trade and they had one quarter in 1954, but in 1962 – eight years later – they had nearly half. Of the increased trade, we have managed to obtain just one twentieth, compared with the nineteen twentieths of the United States and Japan.

Put in yet another way, over those eight years United States exports to the Commonwealth rose by 901 million dollars; E.E.C.'s by 774 million dollars; Japan's by 600 million dollars; and Britain's by 74 million dollars.

Is the right hon. Gentleman proud of that record? Would not he have done better to address himself to these figures and to say what he will do to try to reverse these trends? Why has this happened? First, Government policy has consistently worked against the expansion of Anglo-Commonwealth trade. As I have said, in their doctrinaire rush to re-open speculative commodity markets they cancelled most of the 52 long-term contracts that were in force with Commonwealth countries in 1951. In other ways their commercial policy drove Commonwealth countries into the arms of other suppliers – as when they dismantled a number of important preferences which Australia had enjoyed in our markets. They consistently opposed the negotiation of international commodity agreements which, more than anything else, would have helped to maintain the purchasing power of Commonwealth countries for our exports.

In fact, time and time again they claimed credit for the fall in the purchasing power of these countries for British exports. How often has the Chancellor claimed credit for the improvement in the terms of trade? This is what he means. What else could he mean? The Government's stop-go policy has had a devastating effect on demand for Commonwealth raw materials. The Chancellor always tells us these days how successful he is being in taking up the slack in our industrial system – but who let the slack develop? More correctly – to give discredit where discredit is due – who, by their crash policies in 1957 and 1961, deliberately, and with intent, caused this slack to develop? What did they think this meant in terms of the demand for Commonwealth goods, and hence in the power of the Commonwealth to buy from us? Idle factories, or factories on short time, provide a very poor demand for Commonwealth raw materials.

Without at this point going into the Common Market argument, no one can deny that the deal that they were not only ready but avid to negotiate with Europe, and the undignified political enthusiasm that they showed at their Llandudno Conference, could have any other effect than persuade Commonwealth countries, almost without exception, that the Government were ready to turn their backs on the Commonwealth in favour of their new love.

We made it clear all along that our view is that preferences as such are a much less important asset in inter-Commonwealth trade now, but we were not prepared to sacrifice trade with the Commonwealth in order to get into the Common Market. That was our position and it is our position, and before the debate ends we want to know whether it is the Government's position.

That was the theme of the last Commonwealth Prime Ministers' Conference, when Commonwealth objections were brusquely over-ridden by the Government, and when the Secretary of State for Commonwealth Relations used to the full his not inconsiderable talents with the press, even to the point of direct personal attacks on at least one Commonwealth Prime Minister. The impression they created has remained. This Government's policies have, in a greater or lesser degree, diminished the ability or even, marginally, the willingness of Commonwealth countries to buy their expanding import requirements from us. But there has been another factor at work. Our ability to supply their needs has been diminished because of the Government's economic policy, which has had the effect of building up in this country a soft-centre economy, as opposed to the hard-centre economy needed to produce the machinery, transport equipment, and other equipment which the Commonwealth needs.

A policy which holds down the expansion of our basic industries for three years in every four and then embarks on a frantic consumer goods boom – such as the hire-purchase boom of 1959 – creates an economic structure incapable of meeting the requirements of Commonwealth markets or meeting the ruthless competition of our rivals who have been building up their hard-centre economy, their metal-using industries, over these years. If we seek a symbol of our decline in exporting to the Commonwealth – the right hon. Gentleman never began to get near this point – we need not look beyond the Government's creation of a 'candy-floss' economy in this country.

Thirdly, we have the indifferent effort of so many manufacturers. With a soft home market, they said, 'Why bother?' When producing consumer goods it was easier for them to concentrate on Western Europe. We must ask: what single thing have the Government done in twelve years to encourage direct exports to the Commonwealth? Not even exhortation, though we had a bit this afternoon. In the past, we have had hortatory speeches, many of them very good, about exports to the United States and to Western Europe. But hardly ever about exports to the Commonwealth.

We have had a Dollar Exports Council, which I set up. It is now the Western Hemispheric Exports Council. Why not have a Commonwealth Exports Council? If one tenth of the effort which the Government and industry put into exports to the dollar area or to Europe – a very necessary effort – had been put into a Commonwealth trade drive as well, I should not have been in a position this afternoon to quote the dismal figures which I have been quoting. I hope that before the end of the debate we shall be told that the Prime Minister has thought again and that he now proposes to ask the Board of Trade to encourage the establishment of a really powerful, hard-hitting Council for Exports to the Commonwealth –

Mr Ridley: Why did not you set it up?

Mr Wilson: At that time we were exporting so much to the Commonwealth that our problem, almost, was to have to hold back. I have given the figures. Hon. Members should look at the agreements with other countries. After the war we were extremely short of industrial capacity in steel and chemicals. We had to hold down the export of certain basic chemicals and steel to the

Commonwealth so as to meet our obligations to some other countries.

What do we propose? I will answer that briefly. It is on the record. I am not standing here to announce a belated conversion. I could refer hon. Members to thirty or forty speeches, but I shall not do so. But I welcome the conversion of the right hon. Gentleman to the wider concept of a political and economic community bringing in the Commonwealth and E.F.T.A. That is to be welcomed. I remember that in November 1961, when the Clayton-Herter Report* was published, I said in Leeds that that was the sort of line on which we should be going rather than the narrow line of the Lord Privy Seal.† Last May I summarized our own policy in a ten-point plan. I will stick to the headlines, because many of the things have been argued in detail.

One: arrangements should be made for regular meetings to work through the development and capital investment programmes of each Commonwealth country. We should ask for a specific preference in awarding contracts to Britain – exactly as the United States does in its defence and Buy American Act programmes – from the Commonwealth. I believe that we could get it. I remember that when I was in Canada, the principal utilities, the Ontario Hydro-Electric Scheme, the Toronto subways, and the rest of them, slanted purchasing programmes in the direction of Britain. One province, Saskatchewan, has written into its legislation a 'Buy British' Act awarding preference to Britain, providing that prices are not more than 5 per cent or 10 per cent above prices from other areas. I think that instead of tariff preferences we should have preferences in the way of capital contracts and apply to take part in a Commonwealth development.

Two: in return, we should undertake to provide guaranteed markets for Commonwealth primary produce in this country – never mind the more speculative markets. This would provide assurance and economic stability in the Commonwealth and

*The Report on World Trade by Mr W. Clayton and Mr Chris Herter to the Joint Committee of the two Houses of Congress, 1961.
†Mr Heath.

ensure that our Commonwealth partners were able to afford to maintain and expand their purchases from us.

Three: to fulfil Commonwealth requirements for developmental capital we should agree to expand those sections of our industrial system where existing capacity is inadequate to meet Commonwealth needs – both by incentives to private enterprise and by creating new publicly owned industrial establishments.

Four: we should agree to work jointly for world-wide commodity agreements to stabilize primary prices. The Prime Minister was more forthcoming this afternoon than the Government have been over the last twelve years. He must realize that all the aid supplied by Western countries from 1953 to the present time – all of them, bilaterally and through the United Nations; it has been a considerable figure – has been more than offset by the fall in primary prices over the last ten years.

Five: we should agree to take the initiative with the United States and other friendly countries to expand the volume of world liquidity for financing world trade, with particular emphasis on schemes linking the creation of new credit to the needs of underdeveloped countries and our productive capacity here and in other advanced countries.

Six: I have referred to our programme, a Commonwealth programme, of higher education, which the right hon. Gentleman rightly dealt with this afternoon.

Seven: we should arrange for a fuller exchange of scientific information between countries. I do not think that this has gone anything like far enough.

Eight: we should agree to establish in each advanced country a scheme whereby cities and towns, churches and voluntary organizations, should adopt towns and villages in underdeveloped countries to help them with the provision of industrial and agricultural equipment, school and hospital buildings, and staff, and we should be prepared – make no bones about this – to provide a Government contribution proportionate to the funds raised by voluntary effort.

Nine: we should work towards the creation of a pensionable career service for work in the Commonwealth, irrespective for whom people were working, and provide by legislation that professional and technical experts who take short-service posts in Commonwealth countries should have their pension rights maintained and safeguarded.

Ten: we have exchanged a few words on this matter this afternoon. We should aim to enlist the enthusiasm of young people in a service dedicated to aiding Commonwealth economic and social development.

I wish to refer briefly to one or two points which the Prime Minister made outside the sphere of trade. He referred to aid. I was surprised that he did not give figures for the last year or two. I wonder whether it would be a surprise to him to know that in the first six months of this financial year compared with the first six months of the previous year, according to the figures published by the Government, aid to the Colonies is actually down, and aid to the independent Commonwealth countries is down even more. I hope that we shall hear that this figure is picking up in the second part of the year.

The Prime Minister referred to technical assistance, and we welcome very much what he said about education. Useful work is being done in a limited direction. But, in total, we are playing with it. Let me tell the right hon. Gentleman what we need. A full-scale Ministry of Overseas Development, under a Minister of Cabinet rank, to take over all responsibility for all Commonwealth and other overseas development; to assist and cooperate with voluntary effort in this country – War on Want, Oxfam, Freedom from Hunger, and the rest – and to take responsibility for our representation on the specialized U.N. agencies – F.A.O., W.H.O., and the rest – instead of leaving them as spare-time departments for the Ministries of Agriculture, Education, and Health.

One of the jobs of this Ministry should be to mobilize the unused capacity of this country. What about railway workshops? Would not it make sense to make use of one or two that we are closing down? Many of the older workers are not being re-absorbed in expanding industry. They are going on the dole. Knowing that so many overseas countries are facing a big bottleneck over transport equipment, would not it make sense to turn over one or two of these railway workshops and one or two of the redundant Royal Ordnance factories to this sort of job?

Besides aid in money, what about aid in kind? Would it not be a good idea to work out a few development schemes in which we signed an agreement to supply to these countries 100,000 tons of ingot steel every year in addition to what we are doing for them in finance?

Then, what about scientific research? I hope that particularly as a result of our new university programme we shall find a lot more of our research effort going into the kind of developmental equipment which is designed to help world development. I wonder how many research contracts with universities, colleges of advanced technology, private and public, the Minister for Science has placed for the specific purpose of developing new products of special relevance to food production and the needs of developing countries. We shall not speed the development of hungry countries with the overspill of the affluent society. We may in this country develop a wonderful system of colour television and win export markets for it in advanced countries. Fine, we need those exports; but we need research, also, on all the tools of development which our highly sophisticated civilization has left behind.

I wonder when research was last done on some of the more primitive instruments used in agriculture. Why should not some of our new universities and colleges of advanced technology, in particular, be encouraged to do some of this research and their agricultural departments stimulated into vital life-giving work on plant-breeding, seed-cropping, soil science ecology, and the rest, to raise agricultural productivity? I hope that we shall hear more about that tonight.

The Prime Minister referred to the export of capital and gave some figures. Of course, he did not say for what purposes some of that capital was going. A considerable part of the figures related to oil investment. He is right to say that how much we send abroad depends on the balance of payments position – which at the moment is deteriorating – and on our economic strength, but what we export in the way of investment in the Commonwealth should be more purposefully channelled than it is today. There is trouble in Tanganyika. The Prime Minister has been talking to America about it. I remember crossing swords with the then Chancellor of the Exchequer four years ago about the miserably inadequate aid we were then proposing to send to Tanganyika.

I remember drawing attention to the fact that we seemed to have plenty of capital in this country for property speculation in Manhattan. Some of it has proved singularly unsuccessful and costly to this country, but, successful or not, I was not myself under the impression that the United States was a capital-hungry country, and whatever words one chooses to describe Manhattan one cannot call it an underdeveloped area. I suggest that we shall not get this purposeful channelling of aid where it is needed in the Commonwealth unless we have much more purposeful control of our overseas investment including – I am not burking the phrase – controls on the export of British capital which we can ill spare for the purposes of speculation in the United States of America.

The Prime Minister referred to troop movements in East Africa. Of course, in relation to what has happened there we have fully supported the decision to take up this restrospective 'white man's burden'. We fully echo the tributes to the forces who have fulfilled their task with admirable efficiency and restraint. But our decision to supply their needs has extended still further the stretched resources of our manpower. We had to send troops to four additional Commonwealth countries which none of us even mentioned as possibly requiring to have troops sent to them when we had the defence debate only three weeks ago. If the Prime Minister will permit what I am sure he thinks is an indelicate observation, in Borneo, Cyprus, and the East African countries we have seen the total irrelevance of the Government's obsession with the thermonuclear question. At least it is not totally irrelevant in one sense – that our expenditure on it has sharply diminished our strength in conventional resources.

The Prime Minister said that there is little purpose in going today into questions of Commonwealth machinery, and I agree. The Leader of the House,* in his brief period on his ex-ministerial Elba, had some bright thoughts about a Commonwealth Develop-

*Mr Selwyn Lloyd.

ment Council such as we had in mind in the first of our ten points. We welcomed what he said, but it is a pity that it seems to have been lost sight of. Frankly, in Commonwealth affairs it is the will and purpose that matter much more than the machinery, and in our view it is the will and purpose that have been lacking.

We are appalled at the fact that we have not had the Commonwealth Prime Ministers' conference for three years. In saying that I am trying to forget the disastrous gathering in September 1962, which came near to breaking up the entire Commonwealth relationship. Whatever good had come from all the previous conferences – and I have attended a number and the right hon. Gentleman has attended more – was just about dissipated at that one.

Last November we suggested in the debate on the Address that a Commonwealth Prime Ministers' conference should be held quickly and that one of its purposes should be a Commonwealth discussion of Southern Rhodesia. Even the Secretary of State for Commonwealth Relations flirted with the idea, and no one would ever accuse him of being obsessional about the Commonwealth. I suspect that last week, when the Prime Minister met Mr Winston Field, he was wishing that he had taken our advice and made this a Commonwealth responsibility. I know that when I met Mr Field that thought was uppermost in my mind.

I have one other suggestion which the House might consider – it is for the House, not for the Government or the Opposition Front Bench. The right hon. Gentleman rightly paid tribute to the Commonwealth Parliamentary Association. I wonder whether we could apply all this and go farther. We have had many years' valuable experience of the Council of Europe. Could we not do as much for the Commonwealth idea as Strasbourg has done for the European idea if we were to discuss with our partners in the Commonwealth the idea of a Commonwealth Consultative Assembly, leading to a full Council of the Commonwealth?

Finally, I turn to the relations between the Commonwealth and Common Market in future. The House knows where we stand on this question. It was set out in many debates. It was set out unforgettably in that last speech by Hugh Gaitskell, at Brighton. It was set out in our conference statement and carried by our conference with an overwhelming majority. We said then, and we say now, that we are prepared to resume negotiations for entry into the Common Market if, and only if, we can get the five conditions we then laid down. That position stands.

I repeat, as we said – and supported our statements with our votes in the Lobby – in the debate on 7 and 8 November 1962, that the package deal which the President of the Board of Trade who was then Lord Privy Seal* was in process of completing, did not, in our view, fulfil those five conditions, particularly the one relating to the Commonwealth, when we insisted on

strong and binding safeguards for the trade and other interests of our friends and partners in the Commonwealth.

What we should like is a statement of equal frankness from the Government. I will gladly give way to the Prime Minister if he will answer the question I shall put. I stress particularly that the development since the breakdown of the Common Market talks on the Common Market agricultural policy, with its penal import levies on imports from third countries, including the Commonwealth, reinforces all the anxieties we expressed in the debate on 7 and 8 November 1962 and the debate of 13 December of the same year.

Now I come to the remarkable performance of the Prime Minister on this question. First, we had the singular wording of the Prorogation speech:

My Government deeply regretted the interruption of the negotiations for the accession of the United Kingdom to the Treaties of Paris and Rome.†

The word 'interruption' suggested to some people that not only did the Government deeply regret what had happened, but that they were looking forward to a resumption at the earliest possible moment of negotiations, presumably on the same basis as before.

On 26 October, speaking in Wales, I invited the Prime Minister to say clearly whether he would insist on our five safeguards as a condition for further negotiations about entry. So good were the communications between Pwllheli and Kinross that the Prime

*Mr Edward Heath.
†Official Report, 24 October 1963; Vol. 682, c. 978.

Minister answered this challenge the same evening. I was grateful to him. I felt that his elegantly worded reply was certainly in the very highest tradition of British pantomime. I will read it now and see whether the House does not agree with me. He said this:

> The Common Market opens up an enormous single market on our doorstep. And it is in the interests of our progressive industry and our farmers that we should be a part of this market. But we should only go in if the political and economic terms are suitable. When we applied for entry the terms were not suitable and we stayed out. I do not know if circumstances will arise in which we can open the question again, but if we do we shall still demand the right terms for our entry.

The report goes on in this way:

> Sir Alec added with a smile: 'If Mr Wilson's questions are so easy as that I am going to send him a telegram and ask him to come round the by-election meetings with me.'

It is a pity he did not.

That was his view of what happened in Brussels:

the terms were not suitable and we stayed out.

Is that what he really thinks? He was Foreign Secretary at the time. Did not they tell him anything, either? Did not they tell him about General de Gaulle? I had better explain to him. It was not the Government who said 'No' at Brussels. We were all ready to say 'Yes', falling over ourselves, apparently, to say 'Yes'.

The Prime Minister's account is totally different from that of his right hon. Friend's, because the then Prime Minister, the right hon. Member for Bromley [Mr H. Macmillan], on 11 February, during the inquest into the Brussels breakdown, said this:

> The negotiations did not break down, as they might have done, on a long-drawn-out series of detailed bargains.
>
> If the European vision has been obscured it has not been by a minor obstruction on one side or the other. It was brought to an end by a dramatic, if somewhat brutal, stroke of policy. As I said in my broadcast the next day, the end did not come because the discussions were menaced with failure. On the contrary, it was because they threatened to succeed.*

That was the statement of the then Prime Minister.

*OFFICIAL REPORT, 11 February 1963; Vol. 671, c. 954.

The then Lord Privy Seal, now President of the Board of Trade and Secretary of State for heaven knows what, said this on 12 February:

> The Prime Minister said yesterday, and I said in Brussels, that we were on the point of reaching a concluson to the negotiations . . . with the intervention of the French Foreign Minister, we came to the end of these negotiations.*

I think that that was a pretty fair account of what happened. The Lord Privy Seal was there and he got it about right, but nobody thought of telling the then Foreign Secretary. No; in the dream world that he was living in –

> the terms were not suitable and we stayed out.

I will say this. A few days later the right hon. Gentleman had another go at it and evolved a form of words to which he stuck right through his by-election. I think that he said this seven times, which shows very considerable consistency:

> There is no question of getting into the Common Market before there is a General Election.

He said – [*Laughter*]. No, that is really not fair, because he said something more:

> If the possibility ever occurred in the future it would be for Parliament to decide whether we entered or not.

All right. We accept that it is not likely to come up in this Parliament. But suppose that by a ghastly mischance he and his right hon. Friends get back at the next General Election. I want to ask him this, and to ask him this does not imply that I think that he will get back. It does not imply any morbid preoccupations on my part. The Prime Minister spends half his time going round the country asking me what we are going to do if we win. I am not aware that he regards these questions as conceding the election. Of course, he has not conceded it yet. However, he does get some very full answers from me. The last two questions he put to me got speeches to a total length of 130 minutes at Swansea, for which I apologize.

Now it is my turn. The Prime Minister's answer was that it is a

*OFFICIAL REPORT, 12 February 1963; Vol. 671, cc. 1145–6.

matter for Parliament. What does he propose – a free vote? Is that his idea, that if we get a Conservative Government the decision whether to enter will be taken on a free vote with the Whips off? They were not prepared to do that in 1962. Why, even delegates to their party conference had their arms twisted by a battery of prominent Ministers on the Llandudno Promenade. I read dramatic accounts of it the next day.

I think that we should point out to the right hon. Gentleman that it is usual – he himself may regret it – nowadays, in matters of national importance, for the Government of the day to give a lead to Parliament on these questions and not leave them all to a free vote. Indeed, I may tell him that it is not unknown for the Patronage Secretary* to go to work, for three-line Whips to be issued, and all that sort of thing. Are the Government proposing a free vote on resale price maintenance? Of course not. The Whips will be at work.

So the right hon. Gentleman's answer in Kinross was a complete equivocation. That is why at Birmingham, on 20 January, I gave him another chance to justify his poster-claim of straight talk. I had a reason for doing this at Birmingham on 20 January, because that day, in the *Sunday Telegraph*, I had read these words written by their diplomatic correspondent:

Sir Alec Douglas-Home assured Dr Erhard, the West German Chancellor, in London last week that if the Conservatives win this year's elections his Government would immediately resume its efforts to 'go into Europe'.

That was what the *Sunday Telegraph* said.

The following Friday the *Daily Telegraph* said this:

Mr Butler, Foreign Secretary, yesterday gave Ministers of the six Common Market countries a strongly worded reminder that Britain is determined to join the Common Market and to take an active part in discussions on a European political union.

I personally regard the *Sunday Telegraph* and the *Daily Telegraph* as respectable newspapers – on the news side, anyway. They do not, like some evening newspapers I could think of, dress up some phantasm of one of their political writers and state

*The Government Chief Whip, Mr Martin Redmayne.

categorically that a thing has happened, or that something has been decided, when, in fact, it has not. If the *Sunday Telegraph* says that the Prime Minister said something to Dr Erhard, or if the *Daily Telegraph* says that the Foreign Secretary said something at W.E.U., I believe that they honestly believe it to be true and have substantial grounds for saying it.

So, now, can the House of Commons be told the facts on these things? We had the extraordinary circumstances of the Foreign Secretary at Question Time the other day. Many hon. Members, and at least two leading newspapers, got the idea that he said that there was no question of going into the Common Market. We are used to the Foreign Secretary's statements being interpreted by two different people in two different ways, but not to people hearing it in two different ways. It is extraordinary to see the different recordings of the speech one got in different newspapers. However, we checked in *Hansard* and found that no bones had been broken. All he said was that no question had arisen of our going into Europe.

There is a great deal of confusion about where the Government stand on this matter. The right hon. Gentleman, plainly, has evaded every question put to him on this, but he cannot go on evading it.

Mr Ridley rose:

Mr Wilson: The Prime Minister does not need the hon. Gentleman's protection. He is quite capable of rising and giving us an answer himself. I will gladly give way when he does.

Conscious that perhaps no one has yet told him what my question was, I will repeat it now, across the Table, 'Will he give a pledge that no Government of which he is the head will consider entry into the Common Market on any terms which would reduce Britain's existing freedom to trade with the Commonwealth?'

On behalf of my party, I give that pledge. I put that question to the right hon. Gentleman. The House, and, I believe, the country, will expect an answer.

9   Our National Purpose

A speech made at the Royal Albert Hall on Sunday, 5 April 1964

... In speech after speech, whether in crowded halls or in the House of Commons, which my colleagues and I have made this winter, we have concentrated not on misrepresenting our opponents; not even so much on their record – for that after twelve and a half years is only too well known – but on drawing the lessons from that record. We have concentrated with a frankness and clarity no previous Opposition has ever shown on outlining our policies for the New Britain: our policies for economic policy, for full employment and industrial expansion, for exports, for science and technology, for national and regional planning, for taxation and monetary policy, for housing, for rent policy and security of tenure, for equality of opportunity in our educational system at all levels, for pensions and social security, for a new deal for the under-privileged of the Affluent Society, for our national defence, for our role in the world, for the United Nations, for the future of the Commonwealth, for our part in the war on want, on hunger, and on poverty. No previous Opposition has been so explicit. In 1951 the Conservatives fought the election on three promises – to Mend the Hole in the Purse (it would be unkind to remind them of that), to cut Government expenditure (it has risen by between £3,000 millions and £4,000 millions), and to reopen the Liverpool Cotton Market.

We have stated our policies, and we are agreed on them. With your help we shall make them the policies of our nation. For our people know that the programmes and policies we proclaim are not the cynical prospectus which our opponents used to achieve office in 1951, 1955, and 1959, nor the desperate eleventh-hour conversion of men who have neglected the opportunities of twelve years of unchallenged power and now seek to hide their record behind a smoke-screen of insincerity. They are the application to the world of the sixties and the seventies of basic truths that have inspired this Movement from its earliest days, truths and ideals that express abiding values, but which in their detailed expression are dynamic, urgent, up-to-date, relevant, worthy of a great people.

Every test of public opinion for two years past – polls, by-elections, local elections – has shown the utter and unvarying determination of the British people that it is time for a change. Time for a change, yes, but not in any negative sense. Change of itself has no merit. The change we seek is the change from the drift, and complacency, and self-seeking of these past years, to the assertion of a sense of national purpose, of social purpose, of service to others.

Last October, I was asked to pronounce the last few words of a great Conference. I said:

First, Labour will restore a sense of social purpose and social justice to the conduct of our national life. Secondly, Labour will restore a sense of purpose to Britain's economic and industrial life, based on the mobilization of the energies and the skill and the inventiveness of all our people in the service of the nation. Thirdly, Labour by the exertion of our latent and under-used national strength, by our ability to bring fresh, new, and dynamic human ideas to world affairs, will restore Britain's standing in the world, in the achievement of a new greatness based on the unique contribution we have it in our power to make to the world affairs.

And these are the issues on which we shall be fighting when the opportunity comes. Let me spend a few minutes saying what they are.

1. SOCIAL PURPOSE

We reject the system of values which has been created in twelve years of Conservative rule; a system of values where the spiv, the speculator, the take-over bidder, the tax evader, the land grabber are exalted, and the useful people on whom the welfare, the well-being, of the nation depends treated as second-class citizens. The Conservatives have created a society – indeed, their philosophy has preached the virtues of a society – where, as a distinguished churchman said a year or two ago, the verb 'to have' means more than the verb 'to be'. Those who can make money by a lucky gamble or by exploiting their neighbours through land racketeering are the idols of this new materialism: those who earn money by useful service to the community are at a disadvantage.

The Conservatives preach the philosophy of hedonism. They claim as their own the affluent society. We welcome the rise in living standards of so many of our people: this is what the Labour Party and the trade-union movement were formed to achieve, and we have had a long, hard fight. And over the years, there has not been much doubt whom we were fighting against. And higher living standards have been the rule in other advanced industrial countries, and most of them have advanced a good deal faster than Britain.

But what the Labour Party resents and condemns is the fact that in this so-called affluent society there is still so much avoidable poverty, poverty which is none the less real even though it does not vaunt itself, even though so much of it is hidden behind lace curtains in back streets. Nearly three million of our people dependent on National Assistance for the bare necessities of life, and many more in need of National Assistance but too proud to claim it.

It was the Labour Party that created the Welfare State – Jim Griffiths is with us today. It was Labour who created the National Health Service, an act of great faith, by one of the greatest Socialists who ever lived, at a time when the faint hearts said we could not afford it, and when it had to be pushed through against the opposition of the Conservative Party in Parliament and the country. The inspiration of the Welfare State and its proudest achievement, the National Health Service, was the great Socialist principle – from each according to his means, to each according to his needs.

And that will be the inspiration of the Government which will be formed after the general election. Whatever efforts, whatever sacrifices, may be required to restore this nation to its rightful place in the world, my colleagues and I will ensure that the burdens do not fall where the Conservatives have often placed them – on the backs of those least able to bear them.

Take the individual prescription charges, falling with such inequity on the old and the chronically sick. These were a device of a desperate Tory Chancellor in 1956 facing an economic crisis which his policies had created. Yet, when the last pre-election boom and handouts were contrived five years ago, the removal of this burden, which should have been their first thought, was contemptuously rejected. In the crisis of 1961, prescription charges were doubled, and I have challenged Sir Alec in his present mood of uncongenial liberality to announce that he will scrap these charges now – or justify their continued existence. But the apostle of straight talk remains silent.

Again, when we have demanded, as time and again we have demanded, that the Conservatives should provide more cars for the chronically disabled ex-servicemen, for paraplegic ex-miners and other industrial workers, we have been told that this country – whose economy, Sir Alec claims has never been stronger – would be thrown into bankruptcy by the effort.

Nor shall we solve the great housing problem of our big cities and towns without a fundamental change in social attitudes. The thousands of homeless in London, the hundreds of thousands all over the country living in chronically overcrowded conditions, families divided, young couples fearing to have children lest they are evicted from their inadequate lodgings.

For years, the Conservatives have held down those local authorities anxious to build houses to let at rents that ordinary families can afford. Last year, there were 60,000 fewer council houses built in Britain than Aneurin Bevan achieved in 1948, only three years after the war when shortages of materials and the need to repair war damage – not the meanness of the Chancellor or the ideology of his colleagues – provided the limiting factor. For whereas the Labour Party insists that the people's housing must be a social service, the Conservatives regard it as an instrument for private profit, of rack-renting landlords and property racketeers.

We have extracted from the Conservatives, after repeated challenges, a promise, for what it is worth, that there will be no further decontrol under the Rent Act. But what good is that – they have made it clear that they are relying on the creeping decontrol provisions of the Act, under which every house becomes decontrolled when the tenancy is changed.

The Rent Act, which they promised would solve the housing shortage, has failed. We shall repeal it and replace it by a measure which provides fair rents, and the machinery for settling them, and a guarantee against eviction.

We shall attack the housing problem at the points where it needs to be tackled, first by ensuring that the land will be available at reasonable cost. For land prices in the L.C.C. area have risen from £270 per dwelling in 1951 to £1,550 per dwelling today, and they are still rising. The profiteers' charter which masquerades under the fair title of the South-East Plan will worsen the situation. The only answer is Labour's answer, the public ownership of all urban building land scheduled for new building and redevelopment. In the country generally, total interest charges per house spread over the life of the house have risen from £1,600 in 1951 to over £3,500 today. In the L.C.C. area, of course, the situation is still worse.

A young couple trying to buy themselves a new house today find themselves priced out of the market. Houses in London and the south-east have risen 61 per cent over the past five years, 9 per cent over the past year alone. And the main reason is the rocketing price of land. For them, as for Council tenants, and for ratepayers digging into their pockets to pay the land profiteers' prices, our new Land Commission will be a real protection. So will our proposals for 100 per cent mortgages at reasonable rates of interest. The L.C.C. and other Labour-controlled councils have shown the way, and in the past week, Bill Fiske* has announced Labour's plans for the Greater London Council area.

Housing, education, the children's services, health and welfare, these are the questions which London will decide next Thursday. Combine with a Labour G.L.C. a Labour Government, and you have a democratic partnership which can begin to bring social purpose to our affairs.

*Leader of Labour's campaign in the G.L.C. elections, now Leader of the Greater London Council.

2. ECONOMIC PURPOSE

Labour brought this country through from a fully mobilized war economy to a strongly based peacetime economy by planning and by purpose. For six years under Clem Attlee's administration we led Europe. And for twelve years now, since 1951, we have lagged behind. Other nations, far behind us twelve years ago, have surged past us. Tory freedom, the sacrifice of planning to profit, of production for national purpose to the gamblers' windfall state, have reduced us to an also-ran. Long periods of frustrating restrictions, credit freeze, short feverish pre-election booms which barely survive the counting of the votes.

We shall restore a sense of economic purpose, and we have made clear how we are going to do it. Industrial planning to ensure steady expansion and strength for the pound. We reject the defeatism implicit in the Tory stop-go policy which asserts that this country can expand only for a few months before a rise in imports brings us grinding to a halt.

Sir Alec tells us the economy has never been stronger. His predecessor made the same boast, in exactly the same words, in the 1959 election, and when the figures were produced we found we were running the worst balance of payments since they had last made that boast – in the 1955 election.

The Conservatives have never learnt that the way to a strong economy and a strong pound does not lie in monetary manipulation and slavish adherence to the shibboleths of an outmoded Edwardian financial orthodoxy. Our strength lies in our industry, in a great deal more capital investment, in modernization, in innovation, in scientific research and free play for our technologists and engineers. Last year, we spent out of our limited foreign exchange resources £1,000 millions more than ten years ago on importing manufactured goods that we are perfectly capable of producing for ourselves on a competitive economic basis.

But this means planning for industry. And you won't get it by the polite paper plans of Neddy, or by a system which exalts the money-changers above the practical men in industry who produce the sinews of economic strength. Nor will you achieve success if

Britain's young and unrivalled engineers, and scientists and technologists, designers and craftsmen, production engineers and industrial administrators, are forever held down and frustrated by the boards of directors, far too many of whom owe their place not to fitness for the job but to family, social, and school connexions, or the debilitating intervention of financial interests thinking only of a quick profit for themselves.

Last week there was an article in *The Times* on 'Amateurism in British industry'. I quote:

Money or a title alone still continues frequently to be the sole criterion for election of men (often holding a score or more similar appointments on other boards) who have but the vaguest idea of how the products of their firms are conceived, developed, made, and sold. This is not denying the value of experienced men being brought in. But while the choice of the dilettante director remains a feature of company control, can this be claimed as anything but amateurism?

On the executive side the trained director is the exception and not the rule. It is an acknowledged fact that the calibre of the lower echelons of managers still leaves a lot to be desired.

While the function of private enterprise may be to make a profit, the actual money aspect has an undue, almost naïve, fascination. What else but his money makes the financier or large shareholder such a sycophantically revered and influential figure? While products cannot start to be made without money, not all the bullion in Fort Worth will make a business succeed which does not possess employees of inventive technical ability and productive skill. Yet in practice the materialist outlook unfortunately tends to make money the absolutely dominant force, an outlook that also colours the salary scale, for the farther one gets away from the visible money end, the lower is the reward. As surveys have shown, next to the directors the highest paid group are the salesmen, and so on down the line, with the technical department generally at the end. This unequal reward of ability therefore tends to draw talent away from where it might be best employed. The need for a managerial revolution is widely evident, but the cry seems to have been drowned by deluded murmurs of contentment issuing from behind the closed doors of all too many boardrooms.

Is not that what we have been urging? In a country which a century ago abolished Army Purchase as a means of providing its officers, which has now begun to take cricket seriously enough for even the M.C.C. to abolish the distinction between Gentlemen and Players, we are still prepared to allow too much of British industry, on which alone we depend to prevent this country becoming a second-class power, to be officered from the pages of *Debrett*.

In previous speeches my colleagues and I have set out what needs to be done, our policies for production, investment, exports, for modernizing and energizing the taxation system, for the stimulation of scientific activity, research development, industrial training, for using the power of the State, in partnership with industry, to get a sense of purpose into the nation's production. This will mean priorities. It will mean that the subordination of productive industry to self-seeking financial manoeuvrings must go. The test for us will be purpose.

3. THE RESTORATION OF BRITAIN'S STANDING IN THE WORLD

The Conservatives are prepared voluntarily and complacently to accept second-class status for our country. Loss of influence in the counsels of the nations is the price of economic weakness. And when ten years of Tory freedom were seen to have failed they sought a different escape route – entry into Europe. Whatever the arguments about the Common Market – and our position was firmly and clearly stated in the five conditions we laid down eighteen months ago at Brighton, and in Hugh Gaitskell's great speech there, and it has not changed – the arguments which moved the Tories and the posture in which they applied for entry were no more than a confession of failure.

We are not in Europe. Our economic strength and influence depend on our own efforts, and on them alone, and we believe this country has the skill, and craftsmanship, the power of innovation, and the determination to put forth the efforts that are needed. We reject this defeatism.

Sir Alec tries to base our claim to world status on his borrowed nuclear status symbol, what I recently called his Moss Bros. deterrent. This, he said, ensures our presence at the Council table. And last week, while we sat round the table with sixteen other countries, nuclear and non-nuclear, America and Russia were engaged in bilateral negotiations on the vital question of preventing the spread of nuclear weapons. Britain's bombs provided no ticket to the inner conference room.

When will they learn that this country's influence depends not on nostalgia, or jingoistic speeches, or the waste of thousands of millions on nuclear illusions? It depends on a defence policy based on realism, on the distinctive contribution we can make through our great Commonwealth and naval tradition to the needs of the Western alliance, of the Commonwealth, of collective security through the United Nations.

For a great transformation has come over the world. Even the two great nuclear nations, whose combined destructive power is equal to fifteen tons of TNT for every man, woman, and child on this globe, are having to recognize that their influence is qualified by the acceptance their policies can obtain among 100 nations represented in the U.N., many of which have only recently emerged from colonialist subject status There has never been a time when the world, through the U.N., or the Commonwealth, has looked more anxiously to Britain for a lead, a lead on disarmament – instead of tamely following every American statement – a lead in the attack on world poverty, a positive stand on racial discrimination and racial oppression.

And in place of that lead what do we get – equivocation on the mixed-manned force which stands in the way of an agreement to prevent the spread of nuclear weapons, equivocation on the vital question of nuclear arms for Germany – petulant anti United Nations speeches from the Prime Minister – a long, dismal record of intervention and obstruction with Britain too often ranged on the side of the colonialists and oppressors, Portugal, South Africa, the embattled rulers of the late Central African Federation.

A year ago in Trafalgar Square, I proclaimed the determination of this Party to end the bloody traffic in arms to South Africa. And now, with the U.S. operating a tight embargo, with the U.N. on record against supplying arms to the South African régime, Sir Alec and his Ministers contrive to wriggle and equivocate, condemned by public opinion in this country, by the British Council of Churches, by world opinion. And this is precisely why our influence, whether in the United Nations, whether in the Western Alliance, whether in the Commonwealth, is only a shadow of what it could be and what I believe it will be again.

These then are issues on which we shall be fighting. Social purpose, economic purpose, purpose in foreign affairs. It is our task, for there is no one else to speak for Britain. Four years and more have passed since those days of depression, even defeatism, which followed the election of 1959. Much has changed, not least the mood, the determination of the British people.

We now approach the last weeks of a dying Parliament. But the message we shall take into this fight is one which was given to us in 1959, when this Parliament was only a few weeks old. In his speech to our post-election Conference, the last speech Nye Bevan ever made, he expressed the hopes, the confidence, the determination which have carried this Party through to the eve of victory, and it is with his concluding words I end today:

I have enough faith in my fellow creatures in Great Britain to believe that when they have got over the delirium of the television, when they realize that their new homes that they have been put into are mortgaged to the hilt, when they realize that the moneylender has been elevated to the highest position in the land, when they realize that the refinements to which they should look are not there, when the years go by and they see the challenge of modern society not being met by the Tories, who can consolidate their political powers only on the basis of national mediocrity, who are unable to exploit the resources of their scientists because they are prevented by the greed of their capitalism from doing so, when they realize that the flower of our youth goes abroad today because they are not being given opportunities of using their skill and their knowledge properly at home, when they realize that all the tides of history are flowing in our direction: then, when we say it and mean it, then we shall lead our people to where they deserve to be led.

'When we say it and mean it ... that the tides of history are flowing in our direction, that we represent the future.' In your name, in the name of this great Movement, of countless millions more all over the world, who are watching us, this is what at this great gathering here today, what we say and this is what we mean. This is what we are on the eve of turning into reality.